Vick

Assessing and Supporting Young Children's Learning

for the Early Years Foundation Stage Profile

HODDER
EDUCATION
AN HACHETTE UK COMPANY

> ## Terminology
>
> The term *parents* is used throughout to refer to children's main carer – usually, but not always, the biological parents. As the 2008 EYFS stated: *'Families are all different. Children may live with one or both parents, with other relatives or carers, with same-sex parents or in an extended family.'* The extended family may include grandparents, aunts and uncles, and for some children there may be other combinations too, such as a parent living with a partner who is not the parent and the partner's own children.

Although every effort has been made to ensure that website addresses are correct at time of going to press, Hodder Education cannot be held responsible for the content of any website referenced here. It is sometimes possible to find a relocated web page by typing in the address of the home page for a website in the URL window of your browser.

Hachette UK's policy is to use papers that are natural, renewable and recyclable products and made from wood grown in sustainable forests. The logging and manufacturing processes are expected to conform to the environmental regulations of the country of origin.

Orders: please contact Bookpoint Ltd, 130 Milton Park, Abingdon, Oxon OX14 4SB. Telephone: (44) 01235 827827. Fax: (44) 01235 400454. Lines are open 9.00–5.00, Monday to Saturday, with a 24-hour message answering service. Visit our website at www.hoddereducation.co.uk

First published 2012 by Hodder Education, part of Hachette UK, 338 Euston Road, London NW1 3BH

Copyright © 2012 Vicky Hutchin

Impression number 10 9 8 7 6 5 4 3 2 1

Year   2016 2015 2014 2013 2012

Typeset in ITC Stone Informal Std Medium 11/13 points by Datapage (India) Pvt. Ltd.

Printed in Spain for Hodder Education, part of Hachette UK, 338 Euston Road, London NW1 3BH.

A catalogue record for this title is available from the British Library.

ISBN 978 1 444 17039 9

Contents

Acknowledgements

I would like to give a very special thanks to all the schools and children's centres, practitioners, children and parents who have contributed so much to this book. It is these observations of children, photographs of them actively learning and the children's own mark-making which bring the book to life. A special mention goes to those who also so generously discussed their thoughts about their work with me and provided me with material for the case studies.

In particular I wish to thank:

Pat Davies, Karen Wishart, Jess Snell, Michaela Smith and the staff team, children and parents at Chingford Hall Primary School and Children's Centre, Waltham Forest;

Marcelo Staricoff, Robb Johnson and Michele Connolly, the staff team, children and parents at Hertford Infants School, Brighton;

Joyce Clark, the staff team, children and parents at St Anne's Nursery School and Children's Centre, London;

Ludmila Morris, Annette Rees, Lesley Ferguson and the staff team, children and parents at McMillan Nursery School and Children's Centre, Hillingdon;

Mary Ellinger, Helen Beaumont and the Brighton and Hove Early Years Consultant team;

Andrew Allan at Sir John Cass Foundation School, London;

Peter Catling, the staff team, children and parents at Woodlands Park Nursery School and Children's Centre, London.

A very special thank you to Billy Ridgers, who not only took nearly all the photographs in this book but also read and commented on copious drafts and encouraged me all the way through. This book would not have happened without his unconditional support and time. I would also like to thank Andrew Callaghan for photographs and especially Chas Knight at Hodder Education for his support as my commissioning editor since 1995, when my first book was published by Hodder and Stoughton.

Introduction

From September 2012 a revised Early Years Foundation Stage (EYFS) was introduced in England, building on what has been in place only since 2008. However, the original EYFS itself built on a long-standing tradition in England of child-centred, effective early years practice. This tradition is mirrored in schools and settings across not only England but across the UK, although the requirements and expectations in the different UK countries are not the same.

The revisions to the EYFS brought in many changes, particularly to the statutory assessment Reception teachers are required to carry out at the end of the Reception year. Many teachers, heads and senior management teams are pleased with the changes, feeling that the new systems can help to ensure effective practice is thoroughly embedded and aligned to how children actually learn. They also feel that the revised EYFS will reduce the burden of expectations for assessment placed on early years teachers. But ongoing formative assessment in the early years, as ever, remains based on *observations*: observing what children do, so that teaching can be responsive to the child, is at the heart of effective practice.

The purpose of this book is to explain the *how*, *why* and *what* of *formative* early years assessment and *summative* assessment, including making periodic summaries and tracking progress – plus the summative assessment (the EYFS Profile) at the end of a child's time in Reception. It also provides important information for Year 1 teachers on effective early years pedagogy and how to ensure a smooth transition and continuity of learning for the children as they move on up to Year 1. We need to remember that, in England, statutory school age is the term after a child's fifth birthday. A significant number of children have birthdays in July and August – they will only just be five years old (only 60 months on this Earth!) when they enter Year 1.

Throughout the book there are many wonderful examples of observations and assessments made by professionals – teachers and practitioners – in a number of schools who kindly donated case-study materials for the book. These show *real* young children of four and five, children being themselves: challenging themselves, grappling with new ideas and skills, being actively engaged and thinking, having ideas and enjoying their school life.

Chapter 1 briefly explains the revised EYFS learning, development and assessment requirements, alongside some important findings from research which show the impact of high-quality early years provision throughout children's education. We begin to look at some of the 2012 changes made to statutory assessment in early years which affect schools.

Chapter 2 considers the characteristics of effective learning, highlighted in the 2011 Tickell review which preceded the revised EYFS. These characteristics of lifelong learning are backed by important research on child development, and have been given a renewed focus and higher priority in the revised EYFS, giving us the opportunity to consider the important implications for teaching.

In **Chapter 3**, we move on to look at assessment – formative assessment, assessment for learning and summative assessment – asking: Why do we do it? Do we need it? And is it fit for purpose?

Chapter 4 sets out a set of ten principles for assessment in early years settings, as an aid for schools' and teachers' self-evaluation, when reflecting on whether systems are fit for purpose and how systems can be explained to others, such as parents, governors, inspectors.

Chapters 5 and 6 consider how teachers and practitioners can involve both parents and children – an expectation in assessment in the early years: in fact, involving and informing parents is a formal requirement.

Chapter 7 gets down to the practicalities of observing, assessing and planning. It looks particularly at the Learning Story approach which many schools are now adopting to help them manage formative assessment processes, which at the same time really value children's all-round learning.

In **Chapter 8** the focus moves on to summarising and tracking children's progress, completing the profile and how to support a smooth transition to Year 1.

Chapter 9 rounds the book off with a discussion on data matters. *Does data matter?* And how can we make data fit for purpose in supporting children's learning?

1 Learning and teaching in the early years

In their first five years children develop and learn more rapidly than at any other time in life. The key to effective practice is tuning into the children. It is also what makes working with young children in their very first years in a school or other setting such a delight, working out how best to support each child.

Effective practice means using what you know about each child and responding to this accordingly. In the example below, we will see how the teacher follows the children's interests and lets *them* lead the direction of the activity, whilst she acts as a facilitator, prompting their thinking and problem solving. The example is of a normal everyday event in Reception class of an Early Years Foundation Stage Unit in a primary school, where books and stories take a central role in providing provocations for children's thinking.

Learning and Teaching Story: Jack and the Beanstalk

The children's imagination has been fired by the *Jack and the Beanstalk* story. It all started with one child who wanted the story read over and over again, and then more children became interested too. Using the story as a prompt to new thinking, there are so many directions an exploration or an investigation could go in. The teacher, Jess, started with the children's own thinking. How could a beanstalk be strong enough for a boy to climb? How can the giant stay up in the clouds?

Sara decides to paint a beanstalk.

'Can I see?' asks Gresa. 'I'm going to do one as well.'

'A beanstalk needs to be really tall,' says their teacher, Jess.

So they paint more beanstalks. The children decide they want to make a beanstalk display and go to look for somewhere to put it. Noticing a tall pillar, one said: 'Let's put them up here!' They decide one could go on top of the other.

Jess: *'But how am I going to reach up there?'*

'Get a chair.'

'Get a table,' said the children.

The chair and the table are tried, but Jess still could not reach.

'Get a ladder,' said one of them.

So Jess finds a step-ladder and an adult helped to hold it. The very tall beanstalk is now up, running to the top of the pillar. Then another question arises from one of the children:

'What about the other children? How can they make beanstalks?' asks Gresa.

This is an opportunity for more problem solving. Jess asks if there could be other ways of making beanstalks, instead of painting. They find various sticks and straws and leave them out on a table near the display for others to make. Interest is developing from the other children too – a need for more display space! *'Let's have somewhere to put the other pictures too,'* they suggest.

They move a display board near the beanstalk and another problem arises: the display board is old and needs to look neater. One child suggests covering it in white paper and the other finds a poster of a garden centre – where you can buy beans to plant. And so it continues, with more children becoming involved day by day.

This was a child-initiated idea: the ideas were the children's, but their thinking was facilitated by their teacher, a good listener, willing to let the children's ideas flow and help them act on them. Her suggestions prompted the children to think of alternatives and take the ideas further. She is aware of how children learn, which is succinctly described by Wheeler and Connor (2009) in this way:

> *'Children learn from everything they experience, wherever they are and whoever they are with. The greater the continuity between home and setting and the richer the learning environment in both, the more children benefit.'*

This snapshot of teaching and learning in a vibrant learning community demonstrates that almost anything can be a learning opportunity for the children. If we look at the learning possibilities in this learning event, we would see so many different aspects of significant learning are involved. There is social and emotional learning as the children work together, collaborating and negotiating with each other. They show their understanding of the needs of others, and their confidence in meeting the challenges posed. There are the possibilities for extending their language and communication, expressing their ideas and language for thinking as they communicate with each other and with their teacher. They have creative ideas and find creative solutions, they use their understanding about materials, design and mathematical skills. And all of this was sparked by a literacy event: the reading and retelling of the *Jack and the Beanstalk* story.

In this setting, the staff continually reflect on how successful they are in engaging all the children in learning. The teacher's role is key to the learning that took place: the event became a problem-solving event through her encouragement and open-ended questions. The children introduced many different problems and solved them with support. She allowed the event to flow so that more and more learning came from it. She could have missed this opportunity if she had not listened and observed, and if her planning had not been flexible enough to let it flow. Instead, the children's interest and those of others too was deepened, and their confidence in themselves as active agents in their learning was enhanced.

Recent research on the nature of effective early years practice

The type of early years teaching described above has also been endorsed by some important long-term research carried out in England. This is the Effective Provision of Pre-school Education (EPPE) project, which has been researching the impact of early childhood educational provision on children's development and learning, and future success in school, ever since 1997. More recently it has changed name, to EPPSE (Effective Preschool, Primary and Secondary Education), following the same group of children through to 16+. The research has shown not only that the quality of pre-school provision really matters, but also *which* features of high-quality provision seem to make the most difference to outcomes for children.

The research has followed the educational progress of 3000 children in 141 randomly selected pre-school centres within six local authorities in England from age three to fourteen and beyond. The sample of settings included playgroups, early years classes, private day nurseries, daycare centres run by local authorities, nursery schools and integrated centres. There is now detailed information on the children's progress at age five and at the end of Key Stage 1 (age seven), Key Stage 2 (age eleven) and Key Stage 3 (age fourteen).

What impact does early years provision have on children's later learning?

EPPE has shown that attending high-quality pre-school provision can make a significant difference to children's learning. This was evident at age five, but also continues to be evident nine years on. At age eleven the children who had attended a 'high-quality' setting not only have better educational outcomes, they have also become better learners, more interested in the challenge of learning and, as a result, make faster and greater progress than peers who attended low-quality settings or no setting at all. Children living in disadvantage have most to gain from attending high-quality provision. The research leaves us in no doubt that high-quality provision transforms the child into a more effective learner. Even at age fourteen the impact of attending high-quality pre-school provision is still evident in the children's academic success in maths and science (EPPSE, 2012).

What qualities in early years provision lead to better outcomes?

The EPPE/EPPSE findings shows that high-quality settings – defined as those where outcomes for children were better than all the other settings – have strong leadership, understand the importance of developing a sense of identity for children, and celebrate diversity. These excellent settings included those where children came from significantly socially disadvantaged backgrounds. Practitioners in the settings where children's outcomes were greatest were well qualified, with a high level of understanding of child development as well as a good knowledge of the appropriate early years curriculum. There was good professional development and low staff turnover. Educational aims were shared with parents, and a strong partnership with parents was in evidence.

Effective early years pedagogy

One aspect of the EPPE research, entitled *Researching Effective Pedagogy in the Early Years* (REPEY), reported in 2002, looked in greater detail at the EPPE settings where outcomes for children were highest of all. Their definition of pedagogy takes account of how children learn through everything around them in the early years. It includes the *style* adults adopt as they interact with them, the 'instructive learning environment', the organisation of routines of the day and relationships with families.

Their findings showed that effective pedagogy in the early years involves:

- an equal balance of child-initiated and adult-initiated activities;

- a rich and stimulating learning environment;

- practitioner involvement in supporting children's learning in their self-initiated activities;

- practitioners acting as 'co-researchers', with the children asking open-ended questions to extend their thinking.

This research has been highly significant in England, across the UK and in many other parts of the world, influencing government policy about early years provision. In England it has influenced statutory responsibilities, national guidance materials and practitioners' practice. The first key finding in the list above has had major implications on government policy across the UK, and it is now well established that providing an equal balance of 'freely chosen play activities' and 'teacher-initiated group work' is a key criterion for successful practice.

'In the excellent and good settings the balance of who initiated the activities, staff or child, was very equal, revealing that the pedagogy of these effective settings encourages children to initiate activities as often as the staff.' (Siraj-Blatchford et al, 2002)

The research demonstrated that it was the *style* of adult-child interactions that was important in helping children to learn. Through analysing thousands of hours of tape recordings, they were able to define the nature of those interactions which made the greatest difference. They called these episodes *'sustained shared thinking'*, in which *'both parties must contribute to the thinking and it must develop and extend understanding.'*

'... "sustained shared thinking" was most likely to occur when children were interacting one-to-one with an adult or with a single peer partner. Freely chosen play activities often provided the best opportunities for adults to extend children's thinking.' (Siraj-Blatchford et al, 2002)

As the research has been so influential, let us now look at the policy it has helped to shape.

Policies and principles across the UK

Over the last two decades, education policy changes in the early years in the UK have put the importance of early childhood education on the policy 'radar' as never before. In each country of the UK, 'early years' has become defined as a phase of education in its own right. Even though each country has a different policy and defines its early years 'curriculum' in slightly different ways, there are many similarities in the principles underpinning the policies which build on the idea that teaching needs to be responsive to *how children learn*. This is the kind of teaching in the research described above.

For example, as the Education Scotland website states:

> *'Curriculum for Excellence builds on the solid foundations developed in the critical years of pre-birth to 3 which is supported by the new National Pre-Birth to Three Guidance.*
>
> *'The early level of Curriculum for Excellence spans pre-school and primary as it is designed to meet the needs of most children from 3 years until the end of Primary 1, thus promoting better continuity and progression of learning across the sectors. Many of the core messages of Curriculum for Excellence will already be familiar to early years practitioners, as they relate to the importance of:*
> * *active, experiential learning;*
> * *a holistic approach to learning;*
> * *smooth transitions;*
> * *learning through play.'*

Learning and teaching in the English context

In England, the Early Years Foundation Stage (EYFS) covers what providers, practitioners and teachers need to do right across the age range from birth until the end of the Reception year. The EYFS was first introduced in 2008, providing the statutory framework for all those working with young children, and combining the Framework for those working with under-threes – *Birth to Three Matters* – with the curriculum for children aged three, four and five into a single holistic framework across the birth to five-plus age range. It was revised in 2012, bringing in changes (see below) which built on what went before.

Rooted in principles

The EYFS rests on the firm foundations, not only of the most recent research such as the EPPE and EPPSE projects, but of well established, long-standing effective and reflective early years practice, dating back for generations, to the McMillan sisters and Susan Isaacs in the early twentieth century. It is based on four guiding principles about the uniqueness of every child, the importance of positive relationships between adults and the kind of enabling environment which fosters children's learning and development (Figure 1.1).

A unique child	Positive relationships	Enabling environments	Learning and development
Every child is a unique child who is constantly learning and can be resilient, capable, confident and self-assured.	Children learn to be strong and independent through positive relationships.	Children learn and develop well in enabling environments in which their experiences respond to their individual needs and there is a strong partnership between practitioners, parents and carers.	The framework covers the education and care of all children in early years provision, including children with special educational needs and disabilities.

Figure 1.1 The guiding principles of the 2012 EYFS

Most importantly, the EYFS establishes *child-centred* practice, based around how children develop and learn. The child is seen as *'nested within social contexts'* (Evangelou et al, 2009), first in the family and then beyond this in the setting (or school) that the child attends, and finally in the wider community of which the family and the setting (or school) are both a part.

How children learn underpins teaching in the EYFS and in this way it links closely to the EPPE and EPPSE research. Children learn through initiating their own activities and play, and through positive relationships with parents and practitioners which builds their confidence and self-esteem and a positive attitude to life and learning. The learning environment is key in young children's learning, and setting up an effective learning environment both indoors and out of doors is a vital part of the teacher's role.

The revised 2012 Early Years Foundation Stage

For those familiar with the 2008 EYFS, much in the revised 2012 EYFS remains the same with regard to learning and development – for example, the themes and the continuing emphasis on the need for a balance of child-initiated and adult-led learning opportunities, the importance of the environment and the processes for ongoing assessment. The review process began with the Tickell report, *The Early Years:*

Foundations for life, health and learning, published in 2011. This document placed a greater emphasis on *how* children learn, and using this to guide teaching, as well as on the role of parents in supporting learning.

The revised EYFS also brought in some radical changes. The areas of learning and development changed from six to seven, by separating Communication and Language from Literacy, placing a much improved emphasis on Communication and Language as underpinning children's future success in life. Some of the other areas of learning were renamed and some content realigned, but the most significant change has been to see the areas of learning in a new light, building on an ever-growing understanding of child development. Some areas of learning and development are now identified as **prime areas** and others as **specific areas** (Figure 1.2). You will find the descriptions of all these areas on page 15.

EYFS 2008	Revised EYFS 2012	
	Prime areas of learning	*Specific* areas of learning
Personal, Social and Emotional Development	Personal, Social and Emotional Development (PSED)	
Communication, Language and Literacy	Communication and Language (C and L)	Literacy (L)
Problem-solving, Reasoning and Numeracy		Mathematics (M)
Knowledge and Understanding of the World		Understanding the World (UW)
Physical Development	Physical Development (PD)	
Creative Development		Expressive Arts and Design (EAD)

Figure 1.2 The areas of learning and development

Each area of learning and development is divided into either two or three different aspects, for which each now has one *Early Learning Goal:* a statement which the children should achieve by the end of their Reception year, when most will be aged five. In all, there are now seventeen Early Learning Goals, replacing the sixty-nine previous ones.

The Prime areas of learning and development

The Tickell review highlighted, on the basis of recent research, that three areas of learning were different in nature from others, in that *'Children are primed to encounter their environment through relating to and communicating with others and engaging physically in their experiences'* (Tickell, 2011). These three areas of learning have become the 'prime' areas, as they are fundamental aspects of child development, universal to every child regardless of the social or cultural context.

❝ *These play a crucial role ... in laying the cornerstones for healthy development. Without secure development in these particular areas during this critical period, children will struggle to progress.* ❞

If not supported by adults and *'securely in place by the age of five'*, they are far more difficult to develop later on.

All the areas of learning are interdependent and interconnected, as children do not develop in boxes with subject area headings – their development is holistic and the same goes for learning. In the process of learning one thing, they bring their existing skills, knowledge and understanding to bear on any new learning. However, quite rightly, the Tickell review sees the other areas of learning as distinct from the prime areas.

The Specific areas of learning

The four specific areas of learning are not a natural part of child development. They relate to bodies of knowledge and specific skills that we wish children to learn. They are dependent on children being deliberately given certain experiences to help them learn – as the research that Tickell quotes calls them: *'experience dependent'*. It is important to remember, however, that it is not a question of *first* the prime areas of learning and *then* the specific. Rather, the development of the specific areas of learning begins as we introduce babies and toddlers to a wide range of experiences – such as the world of books and objects to explore. And the prime areas of learning go on developing and remain vital throughout childhood and beyond. *'They grow out of the prime areas and provide important contexts for learning'* (Early Education, 2012). This is quoted from an important guidance document *Development Matters in the Early Years Foundation Stage:* the official non-statutory guidance to support practitioners in their implementation of the EYFS.

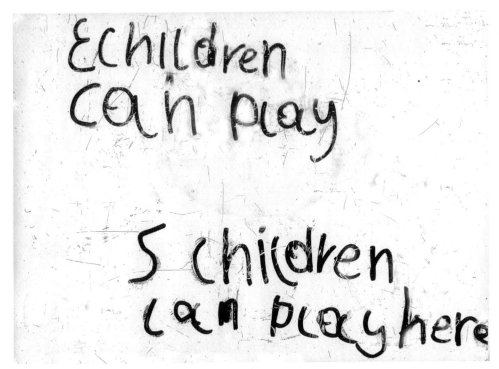

Figure 1.3 Enya, aged 5 years 2 months. Enya's sign for the 'dark tent'. She used a sign in the room to help her spell 'children'. Her sign shows the interconnection between prime and specific areas. Enya is using her skills in literacy to help with managing the class (PSED, a prime area, with Literacy, a specific area).

Mia (in Reception, Autum term)

Mia spent a long time making a monkey puppet. She then pretended it had an accident and stuck masking tape on its injuries. She said to her friend *'Shall we play "monkey is swinging in the trees" and falls out and hurts himself or shall we play "monkey falls out of bed" and hurts himself?'*

This short observation shows Mia thoroughly motivated in a self-directed, child-initiated activity. She has a goal in mind: to make the puppet and use it. In the process her learning covers all three *prime areas of learning*: Personal, Social and Emotional Development, Communication and Language, and Physical Development (to make the puppet); it also covers *specific areas* too: first, Expressive Arts and Design elements, including plenty of imagination. In recalling these two nursery songs, we see how she uses elements of music and literacy. In the process of making the puppet, she undoubtedly also used mathematical skills and her understanding of materials (Understanding the World).

Figure 1.4 Arlie's self-portrait. Expressive Arts and Design is a specific area of learning, but in drawing this he looked carefully at the different features *(Understanding the World)*, used his developing fine motor skills *(Physical Development)* and communicated with others *(Communication and Language)*.

Statutory summative assessment in the early years in England

Although the processes for formative assessment in England remain the same as they have been for very many years, the most radical difference in the revised 2012 EYFS from what went on before is the summative assessment at the end of the early years 'key stage', the Early Years Foundation Stage Profile. The revised 2012 EYFS was the first real change to the Profile for nine years, largely to make it more manageable, whilst keeping it as a holistic assessment of children's learning and development, across all areas of learning. As the Early Learning Goals – the statements of learning that children should achieve by the end of the Reception year – were reduced from 69 in number to just seventeen, the Profile changed too from the previous thirteen nine-point scales to just the Early Learning Goal statements plus a further three aspects of *how* the children have been learning, which we look at in the next chapter. This means there are now just 20 assessment judgements altogether. (You will find the Early Learning Goal statements at the end of this chapter, page 16.)

Developments in assessment processes

This book documents many significant developments that teachers and practitioners are making in their different settings and classrooms to make their assessment processes more fit for purpose, whilst respecting and valuing children's all-round learning and achievements. The *Jack and the Beanstalk* learning event which the teacher, Jess, supported at the beginning of the chapter was based on listening to and observing the children's interests, which she extended by giving them some problems to solve, extending their thinking. It was documented by Jess as a Learning Story, a particularly powerful form of documenting an observation as a narrative (story) which makes it accessible to children and parents and a process which practitioners find easy to use.

The idea of Learning Stories originated in New Zealand, but it has been put to very good use for the UK context. The Learning Story of Sara and Gresa forms part of the records of the two children's achievements, which Jess shares with the children and their parents. It is an important part of the ongoing formative assessment process of the school, which she and the other teachers and practitioners use to inform their planning. You will find explanations of the process and different types of learning stories as you read on.

The most important aspect of formative assessment in the early years is ensuring that children's achievements and learning are truly valued and used to provide the right support. The EYFS sees all children as competent learners '... *who can be resilient, capable, confident and self-assured*'. They can be with our help, and observing children as well as finding out about their learning at home is the key to ensuring our support is right. This useful quote reminds us what we are about when it comes to assessing children's learning:

> '*We need to ensure that what we are measuring truly matters and that we are not simply focusing on things that are easily measured.*' (Bertram and Pascal, 2002)

In the next chapter we look at the characteristics of effective learning – *how* children learn – which have important implications for teaching and for assessment

Reflection

The EPPE research shows that 'freely chosen play activities often provided the best opportunities for adults to extend children's thinking'. How do you plan your time so that you can be involved in and respond to children's play activities?

THE AREAS OF LEARNING AND DEVELOPMENT 2012

The following text is taken directly from the EYFS Statutory Framework, 2012. The Early Learning Goals are reproduced on pages 16–17.

Educational programmes must encompass the following key issues for each area of learning and development:

Prime areas

- **Personal, social and emotional development** involves helping children to develop a positive sense of themselves, and others; to form positive relationships and develop respect for others; to develop social skills and learn how to manage their feelings; to understand appropriate behaviour in groups; and to have confidence in their own abilities.
- **Communication and language** development involves giving children opportunities to experience a rich language environment; to develop their confidence and skills in expressing themselves; and to speak and listen in a range of situations.
- **Physical development** involves providing opportunities for young children to be active and interactive; and to develop their coordination, control, and movement. Children must also be helped to understand the importance of physical activity, and to make healthy choices in relation to food.

Specific areas

- **Literacy** development involves encouraging children to link sounds and letters and to begin to read and write. Children must be given access to a wide range of reading materials (books, poems, and other written materials) to ignite their interest.
- **Mathematics** involves providing children with opportunities to practise and improve their skills in counting numbers, understanding and using numbers, calculating simple addition and subtraction problems, and to describe shapes, spaces, and measures.
- **Understanding the world** involves guiding children to make sense of their physical world and their community through opportunities to explore, observe and find out about people, places, technology and the environment.
- **Expressive arts and design** involves enabling children to explore and play with a wide range of media and materials, as well as providing opportunities and encouragement for sharing their thoughts, ideas and feelings through a variety of activities in art, music, movement, dance, role-play, and design and technology.

THE EARLY LEARNING GOALS 2012

The Prime Areas of Learning and Development

Personal, Social and Emotional Development

Self-confidence and self-awareness: Children are confident to try new activities, and say why they like some activities more than others. They are confident to speak in a familiar group, will talk about their ideas, and will choose the resources they need for their chosen activities. They say when they do or don't need help.

Managing feelings and behaviour: Children talk about how they and others show feelings, talk about their own and others' behaviour, and its consequences, and know that some behaviour is unacceptable. They work as part of a group or class, and understand and follow the rules. They adjust their behaviour to different situations, and take changes of routine in their stride.

Making relationships: Children play co-operatively, taking turns with others. They take account of one another's ideas about how to organise their activity. They show sensitivity to others' needs and feelings, and form positive relationships with adults and other children.

Communication and Language

Listening and attention: Children listen attentively in a range of situations. They listen to stories, accurately anticipating key events and respond to what they hear with relevant comments, questions or actions. They give their attention to what others say and respond appropriately, while engaged in another activity.

Understanding: Children follow instructions involving several ideas or actions. They answer 'how' and 'why' questions about their experiences and in response to stories or events.

Speaking: Children express themselves effectively, showing awareness of listeners' needs. They use past, present and future forms accurately when talking about events that have happened or are to happen in the future. They develop their own narratives and explanations by connecting ideas or events.

Physical Development

Moving and handling: Children show good control and co-ordination in large and small movements. They move confidently in a range of ways, safely negotiating space. They handle equipment and tools effectively, including pencils for writing.

Health and self-care: Children know the importance for good health of physical exercise, and a healthy diet, and talk about ways to keep healthy and safe. They manage their own basic hygiene and personal needs successfully, including dressing and going to the toilet independently.

The Specific Areas of Learning and Development

Literacy

Reading: *Children read and understand simple sentences. They use phonic knowledge to decode regular words and read them aloud accurately. They also read some common irregular words. They demonstrate understanding when talking with others about what they have read.*
Writing: *Children use their phonic knowledge to write words in ways which match their spoken sounds. They also write some irregular common words. They write simple sentences which can be read by themselves and others. Some words are spelt correctly and others are phonetically plausible.*

Mathematics

Numbers: *Children count reliably with numbers from 1 to 20, place them in order and say which number is one more or one less than a given number. Using quantities and objects, they add and subtract two single-digit numbers and count on or back to find the answer. They solve problems, including doubling, halving and sharing.*
Shape, space and measures: *Children use everyday language to talk about size, weight, capacity, position, distance, time and money to compare quantities and objects and to solve problems. They recognise, create and describe patterns. They explore characteristics of everyday objects and shapes and use mathematical language to describe them.*

Understanding the World

People and communities: *Children talk about past and present events in their own lives and in the lives of family members. They know that other children don't always enjoy the same things, and are sensitive to this. They know about similarities and differences between themselves and others, and among families, communities and traditions.*
The world: *Children know about similarities and differences in relation to places, objects, materials and living things. They talk about the features of their own immediate environment and how environments might vary from one another. They make observations of animals and plants and explain why some things occur, and talk about changes.*
Technology: *Children recognise that a range of technology is used in places such as homes and schools. They select and use technology for particular purposes.*

Expressive Arts and Design

Exploring and using media and materials: *children sing songs, make music and dance, and experiment with ways of changing them. They safely use and explore a variety of materials, tools and techniques, experimenting with colour, design, texture, form and function.*
Being imaginative: *Children use what they have learnt about media and materials in original ways, thinking about users and purposes. They represent their own ideas, thoughts and feelings through design and technology, art, music, dance, role play and stories.*

2 The characteristics of effective learning: implications for teaching

As part of the EYFS Profile, in addition to making assessments against the seventeen Early Learning Goals, Reception teachers *must* provide information on how children are learning to Year 1 teachers, to support transition between the Reception year and Year 1. The issue of continuity between Reception and Year 1 has been a longstanding area for development, because teachers have found it difficult to match the EYFS with the primary curriculum. As Julie Fisher put it in her very useful study of transition in 2010:

> 'Anyone walking into an English primary school over the past decade would be forgiven for thinking that the learning needs of 5- and 6-year-olds are very different. While Reception children are found in playful and active learning indoors and outdoors, Year 1 children are found sitting passively on carpets listening to the exposition of their teachers.'

It is a sobering thought that even though children entering Year 1 will usually have spent a whole year in school, approximately one-third of them will only reach statutory school age (the term after the child's fifth birthday) as they enter Year 1. Those with August birthdays will only just have turned five. Continuity in teaching and pedagogy is essential to support continuity in learning. Anything that Reception teachers can do to support smooth transition – by sharing the way that the children learn and how they have developed their pedagogy to match children's learning, keeping them motivated, actively involved and engaged in developing their thinking, skills and understanding – is a good thing!

What are these characteristics of learning?

Play and Exploration, Active Learning and Creativity and Critical Thinking are three of the 'commitments' under the theme of Learning and Development in the 2008 Early Years Foundation Stage. As these are essential aspects of children's learning and development, a strengthened focus was placed on them in the Tickell review, enhanced by more recent research on how children learn. It is information specifically related to these, in respect of each child, that the revised 2012 EYFS asks Reception teachers to provide for Year 1 teachers to *assist with the planning of activities in Year 1'*. However, their importance goes far beyond providing a summary to Year 1 teachers, as they describe the characteristics of lifelong learning and are important for *everyone* involved with young children – parents and practitioners alike.

Each describes a different aspect of how children learn and, for simplicity, each has been divided into three elements, as shown in Figure 2.1.

Playing and Exploring *ENGAGEMENT*	Active Learning *MOTIVATION*	Creating and Thinking Critically *THINKING*
Finding and exploring	*Being involved and concentrating*	*Having their own ideas*
Playing with what they know	*Keeping on trying*	*Making links*
Being willing to 'have a go'	*Enjoying achieving what they set out to do*	*Choosing ways to do things*

Figure 2.1

The non-statutory guidance, *Development Matters 2012*, provides helpful guidance in relation to both children's learning (under the heading of *'A Unique Child'*), and how practitioners might support their learning, in the columns entitled 'Positive Relationships *(what adults could do)'* and 'Enabling Environments *(what adults could provide)'*. Pages 5 to 7 in *Development Matters 2012* give useful information of what practitioners need to do to provide the conditions for each characteristic of effective learning to flourish, through *positive relationships* and *enabling environments*. But in order to understand them more fully, we need to look at some of the research on child development from which they have emerged. To put them into a practical context, let us look first at an example of children deeply involved in learning together through their self-initiated play.

Two four-year-olds are playing in the imaginatively designed wooden playhouse in the trees at the end of the garden. The children call it 'the dark house'. One is collecting sticks, tree bark and dead leaves from outside and piling them up on the tree-trunk table in the house. Outside again, she crouches and pretends to turn on a tap: *'Pretend I was getting a cup of water.'* With two sticks in her hand, she moves quickly back into the house and says: *'I am lighting it. I'm lighting the fire. It's done!'* She runs outside to where the other girl is standing, looking intently at the roof. *'Look, there's a leak on the top of the roof!'* They both run in again: *'Can we put loads of lighters here? You see the big bad wolf! I can see his feet now! He's going to pop out of the chimney as quick as he could! Oh! The wolf is climbing down! He's falling in the pot of water!'* *'Light, light, light!'*, she says as she waves her sticks over the pile of leaves, sticks and bark under the imaginary pot.

The intensity of the collaboration and joint imagination of these two is wonderful to behold, and continues for much of the morning as ideas flow between them. As the observation was of just one of the children, we mainly hear one side of the conversation here, but they are both completely absorbed in developing the storyline, re-enacting a traditional tale in their own way, using every aspect of the natural environment available to represent their play.

What were these children learning and what skills, knowledge and understanding did they bring to the play? In relation to the characteristics of learning, what are these two children doing as they re-create and act out this story together? The day before, the children had been read the story of the Three Little Pigs at the group story time, but it is not part of a class 'theme' or topic. For one reason or another these two had chosen, with no prompting from adults or other children, to act out the story for themselves. Throughout this chapter we shall refer back to this rich episode of play.

Playing and Exploring: *Engagement*

The EYFS Statutory Framework, 2012, makes play statutory:

> ❛ *Each area of learning and development must be implemented through planned and purposeful play and a mix of adult-led and child-initiated activity. Play is essential for children's development....* ❜

Vygotsky was well aware of the importance of play in children's learning. In play, children operate at their highest level *'beyond his average age, above his daily behaviour; in play it is as though he were a head taller than himself'* (Vygotsky, 1978). Play is so important to children's learning and – whether a child is in Nursery, Reception or Key Stage 1 – it needs to be taken very seriously. Although children *can* learn and develop 'at their highest level' through play, we need to make sure we are providing the best conditions for their play to flourish.

The *Early Years Learning and Development Review*, published in 2009 as an important aspect of the EYFS review, puts the importance of play and the role of practitioners in supporting it as one of its main findings:

> *'Play is a prime context for development...there are now studies on different kinds of play, especially the ways it can be enriched by guiding, planning and resourcing on the part of staff in settings.'* (Evangelou et al, 2009)

Much of the recent research looks at the importance of play on brain development.

Play is not 'for real' and the children can decide to move in and out of play at any point, or repeat it as much as they like. Vivian Gussin Paley has some important messages for us about the importance of fantasy play in building confidence and positive dispositions:

> *'Fantasy play, rather than being a distraction, helps children achieve the goal of having an open mind.'* (Paley, 2004)

Play provides children with the opportunity to:

- try out what it might feel like to be another person (mother, father, baby, brother, sister) or another creature (a dog, cat, crocodile, etc);
- make decisions and choices and try out what it is like to be in control;
- practise existing skills and knowledge in new ways;
- apply skills and knowledge which are in the process of being learnt and developed;
- learn to negotiate and try out new ways of relating to others;
- manage feelings which may be frightening or enjoyable;
- devise problems and be the one who solves them;
- put developing language and communication skills to new uses.

The two girls in the example are certainly involved in rich play together. Their play has been enriched by the story reading the day before, the environment, and the time and space they have been given to play. We can see how each element of this EYFS characteristic of learning is demonstrated in their play.

Finding out and exploring

'*Finding out and exploring*' results from children's '*innate curiosity*' and provides the experiences '*from which children build concepts, test ideas and find out*' (Tickell, 2011, p.89). We all use this type of exploration when involved in something new, as if we are asking ourselves: '*What is this?*' and '*What does this do?*', followed by '*What can I do with this?*' The more opportunities to explore and try things out in different ways, the better we become at solving problems.

Figure 2.2 Providing interesting things to explore, tapping into children's innate curiosity.

In the case of the two girls described on page 20, their explorations are slightly different from the exploratory play described in the Tickell review. The girls are exploring their own imaginative ideas as well as the imaginative possibilities in the story. They are deeply involved in exploring the story in their own way, their emotions, the sequence of actions in the story, and how they can make use of their environment to enhance it.

Playing with what they know

The Tickell review stated that this element of 'Playing and Exploring' *'describes the importance of play as a context to bring together their current understandings, flexibly combining, refining and exploring their ideas in imaginative ways.'*

Tina Bruce often calls play 'an integrating mechanism'. *'Play ... is about how children begin to try things out and make sense of what they have been learning and put it to use'* (Bruce et al, 2010).

As they grow and develop, so too do children's abilities to imagine, and in the example of the two girls we can see how the story sparks off rich imagination. They are pretending that the objects they use are other things and in so doing use what they know about 'lighters', or leaking roofs, water, fire, the wolf and the language of story. They are certainly playing with the story, re-presenting their knowledge of the story as they re-enact it, taking on roles where they are the key players in catching the wolf. Most of all in this play they are completely *in control* of what goes on.

Being willing to 'have a go'

Confidence and positive dispositions about oneself and one's own abilities to learn, be and act lies at the heart of 'being willing to have a go'. This enables us (children and adults) to initiate activities, challenge ourselves, take risks and make mistakes. And nothing could be better than play in providing these opportunities for children. *'If children have many positive experiences of, for example, trying things that are difficult in a safe environment, they will develop the habit or "disposition" of persevering with difficulty when they are in another environment'* (Carr, 1998).

In the observation, the two girls are very willing to 'have a go', each contributing to the story as they develop it together. This shows not only initiative but being willing to engage with each other, taking a risk that your own idea may be accepted or rejected by the other person.

The adult role: promoting play and exploration

In play and exploration the child is completely in control of the play, the exploration and their own learning: the child is 'leading the learning'. They can choose when to start and when to stop, the theme, what will and won't be involved. Learning is just like this – we cannot learn for another person. The learner is in control of their own learning.

Adult support can prevent play from becoming repetitive or stuck, beginning by observing and becoming a partner in the play, taking on a role allocated by the child, while ensuring the rules about what each character can or cannot do are the child's. In the case of the two children in the example, there was no need for adult support and it may have interfered with the flow. But the event was well worth observing, finding out the effective learning the story had provoked.

Active Learning: *Motivation*

Active learning means being mentally active and alert. The EYFS commitment states that *'Active learning involves other people, objects, ideas and events that engage and involve children for sustained periods.'* In the Tickell review, active learning was described in this way:

> ❝ This strand highlights key characteristics which arise from intrinsic motivation to achieve mastery – to experience competence, understanding and autonomy. ❞

The first element of active learning is to do with involvement and concentration. The children in the observation at the beginning of the chapter are deeply involved in their activity for a *'sustained period'*. They are totally absorbed and motivated by their joint goal, persisting in acting out their story.

Being involved and concentrating

Intrinsic motivation is the key to concentration, but what motivates one person will not be the same as what motivates another. It could be social and emotional reasons such as wanting to make friends, or cognitive factors, such as understanding an idea or wanting to know how something works. It involves *'the intensity of attention'* children may give when *'following a line of interest'* (Tickell, p.90). Research shows that when children are able to make their own choices, follow their own train of thought and make use of their natural curiosity, they are much more likely to become deeply involved and concentrate. This is why playing and exploring are so motivating for children, and why 'child-initiated' activities are so important.

The concept of involvement

Ferre Laevers, whose work has been very important internationally in influencing self-evaluation processes for schools and settings, believes that when children are deeply involved in what they are doing, significant, *deep-level learning* is taking place: *'an involved person is driven by his exploratory need which puts him in a state of mind favourable for deep-level learning'* (Laevers, 1994). Deep-level learning involves challenge, pushing ourselves beyond our current skills and understanding towards something new. It allows us to figure something out so that we change the way we think about it, grasp a new idea or grapple with a new skill.

> *'When children are concentrated and focused, interested, motivated, fascinated, mentally active, fully experiencing sensations and meanings, enjoying the satisfaction of the exploratory drive, operating at the very limits of their capabilities, we know that deep-level learning is taking place. If deep-level learning is taking place, a person is operating at the limits of their "zone of proximal development".'* (Laevers, 2000)

Keeping on trying

Persistence, particularly in the face of any challenge or difficulty, is a key aspect of learning. Carol Dweck's research has helped us to understand why some children (and adults) might give up easily and others seem to enjoy any challenge and persist at it.

The views we have of ourselves as learners has a huge influence on how we are as learners and on our lives in general. Dweck shows that children's views about themselves as learners begin to be formed at an early age. They develop a mindset that will either help them in their ability to learn or will hinder it. Her theory refers to two mindsets: the *fixed* mindset and the *growth* mindset. Those with the fixed mindset believe that their abilities are fixed and cannot be changed. *'People are all born with a love of learning, but the fixed mindset can undo it'* (Dweck, 2006). They have a tendency to want to get things right, because if they don't, they will feel a failure. People with a fixed mindset are unlikely to want to take on challenges they are unsure of, preferring to be in the safety zone of what they know they can achieve.

Those with the *growth* mindset are excited by challenge – they push their own boundaries and are motivated to find a way around obstacles. They believe ability is not fixed, but can grow and develop.

> *'As soon as children become able to evaluate themselves, some of them are afraid of challenges. They become afraid of not being smart.'* (Dweck, 2006)

One experiment with four-year-olds offered them a choice of puzzles: they could redo an easy puzzle they had already done or try a harder one. The children with fixed mindsets wanted to redo the puzzles, the growth mindset children were up for the challenge of the harder puzzles.

Dweck believes that in part it is the influence that adults' views have on the child – for example, having the 'good' end product, rather than focusing on the *processes* involved in doing something – that causes the fixed mindset problem. Inadvertently we can limit children's learning by limiting their drive to try things which challenge them. The messages we give are crucial: '*It can be a fixed mindset message that says: You have permanent traits and I'm judging them. Or it can be a growth mindset message that says: You are a developing person and I am interested in your development.*'

The way we praise children can be the root of the problem. Praising a child for their cleverness or intelligence may be done to try and boost confidence, but is more likely to result in developing a fixed mindset, with the child seeing little point in persisting in the face of difficulty. However, praising children for their *efforts*, what they accomplished through practice, persistence or trying out different strategies, will help to develop a growth mindset.

'When we receive encouragement for our efforts and our ideas are valued, our feelings acknowledged and our discoveries recognised, we come to see the world as a safe place, and ourselves as competent and capable agents within it. These positive messages give us the confidence to take on the risks and challenges that all new learning brings. We become keen to learn, challenges are welcomed and failures are simply seen as opportunities for further problem solving and exploration.' (National Strategies, 2007)

Enjoying achieving what they set out to do

Persistence and being willing to have a go both involve the child in having some kind of goal in mind. Success in achieving it brings satisfaction. There are different types of goals: those that come from within, linked to our internal 'intrinsic motivation' *(mastery goals)* and those which are motivated by external incentives or rewards *(performance goals)*. Performance goals may have a short-term effect, in order to get the reward, but as Nancy Stewart (2011) points out: '*Not surprisingly, researchers find that the mastery goals consistently support people to learn and perform at a higher level than the performance goals.*' As an example, one of the pieces of research she quotes shows that when children '*expected and received a ribbon and gold star for drawing pictures, they later spent less time on the activity*'.

Of course adults also have goals that they want children to achieve. If the child is only doing something to please the adult, the motivation will not last. The children need to understand the goal and the benefits

Figure 2.3 A goal-oriented self-chosen activity

to be gained from it, if they are to make it a goal of their own. This has implications for how we explain the purposes of any adult-led activity and makes us aware about the impact of how we reward children.

The adult role: promoting active learning

The EYFS and the EPPE research talk about the need for a balance of child-initiated and adult-led activities. For child-initiated learning, a stimulating learning environment with novel as well as familiar things to explore, building on children's interests, and allowing plenty of time to do it, is bound to motivate the children. As Nancy Stewart (2011) says, *'Choice, time and space, freedom to follow ideas without anxiety about an end product'* is important.

Adult-led activities can support learning by ensuring that any planned activity is based on things that children will be interested in, and is at the right level of understanding and challenge for them, playful and flexible enough to enable the children to become deeply involved, and make the activity 'their own'.

Creating and Thinking Critically: *Thinking*

The most important aspect of learning is not the specific knowledge or the facts that we teach children, because these rapidly become superseded by more up to date ones. Skills such as becoming literate and being able to calculate are of course essential skills, and so is learning how to learn. What children need as they grow up in this fast-changing world is the ability to deal with new situations, and a key aspect of this is developing self-awareness. This is where creativity and critical thinking come in. Supporting children to develop their critical thinking skills can be among the most rewarding aspects of working with young children, becoming co-researchers alongside them.

Creativity involves seeing things in new ways, making new connections, using imagination to develop thinking and generate new ideas. *'All people have creative abilities.... When individuals find their creative strengths, it can have an enormous impact on self-esteem and on overall achievement'* (Robinson, 1999). This does not mean ideas that no one has thought of before, but new ideas and new ways of thinking for this particular child. As the Tickell review put it:

❝ *Being inventive allows children to find new problems as they seek challenge and to explore ways of solving these.* ❞

Thinking critically involves developing the kind of reflective thinking which helps us to organise our thoughts and think things through. It involves reflecting on and developing awareness of one's own learning and developing metacognition – 'learning how to learn'.

Nancy Kline's research has shown the importance of the 'thinking environment' for adults to improve their thinking skills. Her research shows that we rarely provide the type of environments for thinking and creativity to flourish.

> 'The best conditions for thinking are not tense. They are gentle. They are quiet. They are unrushed. They are stimulating but not competitive. They are encouraging. They are ... both rigorous and nimble.' (Kline, 1999)

Creating a 'thinking environment' begins by listening attentively to each other. Think of the number of times in a conversation that someone else talks over you or finishes your sentence for you. This is because you have sparked off their own thinking, and they are no longer listening to you! This happens with adults talking to adults, but it happens even more when we talk to children, going hand in hand with the tendency to ask them lots of questions, most only requiring one-word answers. None of this helps children to use their imaginations, think about possibilities and have new ideas or figure things out for themselves. Enabling children to think critically means improving the thinking environment, ensuring it is stimulating, with interesting things to discover, explore and provoke children to ponder on and – most importantly – the time and encouragement to do so.

Having their own ideas

Returning to the girls we saw deeply involved in imaginative play together at the beginning of this chapter, the girls chose to play in this way – generating their own ideas, making the story their own. They are being inventive.

Making links

In the Tickell review, this aspect of creativity and critical thinking was called *'using what they know to learn new things'*. The EYFS commitment card 4.3 in 2008, still part of the non-statutory guidance, stated:

❢ *When children have opportunities to play with ideas in different situations and with a variety of resources, they discover connections and come to new and better understandings and ways of doing things. Adult support in this process enhances their ability to think critically and ask questions.*❢

Being able to reflect on how we came up with particular ideas or new ways of seeing something is important.

Choosing ways to do things and finding new ways

This final aspect of creating and thinking critically involves *'making choices and decisions about how to approach a task, planning and monitoring what to do, and being able to change strategies'* (Tickell, 2011). Research shows that when children are involved in their own self-chosen activities, they are more likely to want to find the right strategy than if it is adult-directed. Encouraging children to investigate and experiment gives them the experience they need to begin to organise their thoughts and figure out how to proceed.

Some of the most important skills children need for the future are the *metacognitive* skills which involve them in reflecting on their learning. Recent research has shown that when children are asked *how* they solved a problem, they learnt more than when they were just given positive feedback on solving the problem (Evangelou et al, 2009).

The adult role: promoting creativity and critical thinking

A child who is not given the opportunity to think, play, explore investigate and find and solve problems is far less likely to be a resilient, creative learner willing to have a go, persist, or think critically.

Supporting the development of thinking skills requires a particular style of interaction on the part of the adult – thinking alongside the children in a joint enquiry, asking open-ended questions and setting up ways to find answers and investigate together: being a co-researcher. For the adult, this is where sustained shared thinking, discussed in Chapter 1, comes into its own. As Marion Dowling (2005) says in her work on sustained shared thinking, practitioners need to be: *'able to enter the child's world, recognise his/her interests, dilemmas and concerns and have a conversation which encourages further thinking.'*

Conversations about the learning processes children are using are important in helping them to develop awareness of their own learning, using open-ended questions such as *'How did you manage to do that?'* or *'What helped you do that?'* We do not hold these types of conversations nearly enough with children in the early years or in school. At first children who are not familiar with this way of working may need us to help them become aware of the skills and knowledge they have applied, through talking with them about what we have seen them do. Sharing something about your own learning is also helpful: *'I really have to think about that'* or *'I am not sure, I wonder how to do that? I will need to find out more.'* Often children spark ideas off each other too, as they each add their own views.

Assessing *how* children are learning

We began this chapter by discussing the fact that the EYFS has made assessing *how* children learn a statutory task for Reception teachers. Although Reception teachers are asked to provide a summary of learning over time, it is useful to examine specific significant examples, to draw out how the child or children demonstrate particular learning characteristics.

Threaded throughout this chapter was information about how the two girls playing were also learning. Figure 2.4 provides a summary of what we found out.

Characteristics of learning: *What does the analysis of the learning show?*
Playing and exploring: *finding out and exploring, playing with what they know, being willing to have a go.*
In re-enacting a familiar story the girls were incorporating not only their knowledge, skills and understanding of the story, but also about cause, effect and their technical knowledge of materials. They have the confidence to 'have a go' together.
Active learning: *being involved and concentrating, keeping on trying, enjoying achieving what they set out to do.*
The girls were deeply involved together for a sustained period, at least half the morning session. Play was self-chosen and self-motivated.
Creating and thinking critically: *having their own ideas, making links, choosing ways to do things and finding new ways*
They used their creativity to recreate the story together in their own way, applying imagination to find a new way to retell the story, making links between what they already know.

Figure 2.4

In the observations and evidence of learning in the examples in the next few chapters you will see how, as part of the analysis, each includes some comment about what the observation shows about how the child is learning, using the characteristics of learning.

Some significant achievements in the Reception year

A powerful provocation for children's learning introduced in this Reception class is the use of stories which are read to the children at least twice a day. After one or two stories about dragons for Chinese New Year in the Year of the Dragon, and acting out the Lion Dance with the dragon the children had created, their teacher, Robb, asked the children to make up their own stories about dragons. They were asked to think of the story in three phases, so that each had a beginning, middle and end. First the children drew their first pictures, then dictated the first part of their stories.

The other two parts of the story were completed on the following days, helping the children to experience sequencing their own story and how to end it. The learning was ongoing and sustained, with plenty of time for the children to review what they had done and discuss it with a member of staff before completing the next part of the story. The results were some highly imaginative stories.

The stories show how the teacher's learning intention was met because it was creative and built on the children's imaginations, already fired by other experiences. The children were provided with an opportunity to compose their own story. Because the stories were scribed for them, the children could concentrate on the purpose: to tell a good tale, freeing up their creativity and imagination. In this way the children have:

- explored new ideas and had a go at composing a story with a beginning, middle and end;

- played with what they have learnt about dragons and traditional stories, using their own knowledge in their own unique ways;

- become involved in something which has interested them, persisting with it to achieve their own self-motivated goal;

- engaged in creative thinking, using their critical thinking skills.

At the end of this chapter and several others you will find a dragon story. We start with Louis's.

Reflection

The next time you write down an observation of a child, think about *how the child is learning*. Try using the format in Figure 2.4: does this help you to become familiar with how the EYFS perceives the characteristics of effective learning?

Louis's dragon story

Once upon a time there was a Chinese dragon. It chased me and Aiden all the way to Australia.

Then me and Aiden got away from the Chinese dragon and we ended up in some woods and we hid behind some trees in case the Chinese dragon found us.

Me and Aiden ran into a house. The Chinese dragon smashed the door down. I pushed the dragon so hard I pushed him through the sea all the way to India and then to the end of the world.

3 Why do we need to assess children in the early years?

When we use the word *teach*, we tend to think of a formal process whereby a person imparts knowledge to another or gives instructions on how to do something. But this formal process does not relate to how young children learn. There may be a specific body of knowledge and skills or curriculum which we want children to learn, but unless we start with what the children already know and can do and how they learn, our teaching will miss the mark.

Tailoring teaching to children's learning

For many children, coming to an early years setting or class is likely to be the first time the child has been in a group with so many peers of the same age. Each child is unique and different, and brings with her/him a unique set of experiences and achievements, largely based on her/his life at home.

> By tuning in early to the range of strengths, interests and passions of children as they begin to emerge, practitioners can gain an insight into their potential and plan opportunities that enable this to be celebrated and nurtured.

(National Strategies, 2010)

Teaching needs to be tailored to each unique child if it is to be successful in extending learning. It needs to address *how* young children learn. This means it must be based on the needs, interests, preferences and capabilities of the children. And the only way to find this out and meet their learning needs is through observing them and talking to those who know them best – their parents.

This is the starting point for teaching – not a specific body of knowledge or set of instructions to be imparted or a fixed curriculum, but these children, here and now. This point is backed up by the REPEY research discussed in the last chapter. One of the key findings of the REPEY (2002) research is that: *'The more knowledge the adult has of the child, the better matched their support and the more effective the subsequent learning.'*

As a Reception teacher and Early Years Foundation Stage Coordinator explained:

> *'It's no use starting with the curriculum – children don't learn in curriculum areas or boxes. This is a simplistic view of learning which doesn't relate to the reality. It doesn't tell us what we need to know. We need a record of the whole child, so to find out we focus on the children's own child-initiated learning – what they choose to do independently of us.'*

Of course, we also need an idea of what we wish them to understand and be able to do. This is the long-term plan – the overall entitlement for every child. But effective teaching doesn't impose, it responds to how each child is learning as well as where they are in their learning. It is dependent on looking at each child's learning, and assessing it in order to decide what opportunities to provide next.

This is where assessment comes in. When evidence is gathered about the child's learning, an assessment or judgement is made: *What is this evidence telling us?* The answer to this question has direct implications for what happens next: *What can we do to extend their learning?*

The role of assessment in effective teaching

In order to extend a child's development and learning, key questions need to be asked:

- How does this child respond in different situations?

- What sort of things interest and absorb her/him?

- In what situations does she/he show most confidence?

- What skills and understanding are already in evidence?

- What does she/he appear to find challenging, difficult or frustrating?

And in the light of what we know about this child:

- What can we do to further her/his development and learning?

Effective teaching depends on knowing the children. We need to assess children's learning and development so that we can plan appropriately for them, to ensure that children are making progress. As the EYFS 2008 says:

> *All planning starts with observing children in order to understand and consider their current interests, development and learning.*

Unless we regularly observe children, we will not know if our provision for them is right or what to do next to extend this. The richest source of information about their learning will come from observations of children at play and in their self-chosen activities.

The example below shows this in action. The teacher uses what she has found out about the child's interests and skills to tailor her teaching into an exciting, motivating learning event.

Frankie is four years old and in a Reception class. He has shown some interest and excitement about letter sounds and matching words that rhyme: 'Dog and fog! That matches!' he said excitedly one day early in the Autumn term.

A few days later he went over to his teacher and said as he points to the musical instruments: 'I need a song about golf, using those.' His teacher replied: 'How about we use a song we already know and change the words?' Frankie agreed that this might work and together they created a new song with Frankie finding words that rhyme, such as roll and hole. Later he sang the new song to the whole class.

His teacher had picked up his interest in sounds in words, particularly in how rhyming words are created by keeping the sound the same at the end of the word. She was able to use this information in how she supported him a few days later. There are also many observations showing his interest in a variety of sporting activities.

The role of parents in assessment

An important reason for observing and making assessments is to share with parents what we are finding out about the child. We also need to *involve* the parents too: they know their children best and what they see their children do at home is important. Putting the 'evidence' from parents with the 'evidence' from practitioners in the setting together, we are able to develop a fully rounded assessment, showing the child's achievements holistically. This helps us to get the planning right.

Often other professionals need to be involved in supporting the children to develop and learn, such as health care professionals. Practitioners' and parents' observations and assessments have a vital role together in informing other professionals about the child.

Different types of assessment

It is important to distinguish between different types of assessment, in particular the **ongoing formative assessment**, the type described above, which *informs* teaching and is therefore a core part of the teacher's role, and **summative assessment**. Shirley Clarke (2001) describes the differences between different types of assessment in the following gardening analogy:

> '...if we think of our children as plants ... **summative** assessment of the plants is the process of simply measuring them. The measurements might be interesting to compare and analyse, but in themselves, they do not affect the growth of the plants. **Formative** assessment, on the other hand, is the garden equivalent of feeding and watering plants, directly affecting their growth.'

Formative assessment is designed to extend learning by tailoring teaching. On the other hand, summative assessment is an assessment of the child's performance at a point in time. Summative assessment *'is static and one-way (the teacher or examiner usually judges the pupil). Whereas formative assessment is ongoing and dynamic...'* (Assessment Reform Group, 2009). The main difference derives from the *purpose* to which the assessment is put.

Summative assessment should also be used to inform teaching, particularly when it is used to track a child's progress over time. However, as it is less immediate and 'dynamic' than formative assessment, it informs teaching in a more general way.

Formative assessment

The important point about formative assessment is that it is *'built into the learning process'* (Assessment Reform Group, 2009), a central part of pedagogy. Over the last fifteen or more years, formative assessment as a core aspect of teaching has increasingly taken centre stage right across education. The work of Paul Black, Dylan Wiliam and the Assessment Reform Group has been significant in this history. Their research on formative assessment has shown that making good use of assessment information with the pupils in the classroom to promote learning raises achievement. As Dylan Wiliam said, in discussing his review of the research into the effect of formative assessment on outcomes for pupils:

> 'What is intriguing about the research on formative assessment is that whether the focus of the study is Portugal or the United States, whether it is looking at 4-year-olds or 24-year-olds, whether it is looking at music or mathematics, there appears to be consistent, substantial effects.' (Wiliam, 2009)

Observing: gathering evidence of learning in the early years

Assessment processes in the early years have always involved *observing* children, as the main way of gathering evidence of children's learning. It is one of the most powerful tools in the early years practitioner's tool bag, an essential component of assessment *for* learning in the early years, ensuring that the provision made and the adult's own role within it supports and extends children's learning. It is not like assessing older children: there is very little mark-making or written samples that can be 'marked', and this would only give an extremely limited assessment of the child's real abilities. *Observation* is the key to finding out.

6 *Observing and listening carefully to the voices of the children will reveal insights into their learning and development that could never be captured through more formal assessments.*9

(National Strategies, 2010)

As the 'Effective Practice' section of the 2008 EYFS on observation, assessment and planning put it: *'Without observation, overall planning would be simply based on what we felt was important, fun or interesting (or all three) but it might not meet the needs of children in our care.'*

Observation is as important now as it has been in the past, and has been reiterated in the revised EYFS Statutory Framework:

❛ Ongoing assessment is an integral part of the learning and development process. It involves practitioners observing children to understand their level of achievement, interests and learning styles, and then to shape learning experiences for each child reflecting those observations. ❜

(EYFS, 2012)

Observing play

Thoughtfully made observation by experienced practitioners who know what to look for reveals a wealth of useful evidence for assessment purposes. The most important observations are those made on children in play and their own self-chosen, self-initiated activities, as this is where children's learning is at its most intense. As the 2008 EYFS states, relating back to Vygotsky (1978): 'In their play children learn and develop at their highest level' (EYFS Commitment Card, 4.1). And as the important *Early Years Learning and Development Review*, reiterated:

> 'Play is a prime context for development... there are now studies on different kinds of play, especially the ways it can be enriched by guiding, planning and resourcing on the part of staff in settings.' (Evangelou et al, 2009)

Young children of Nursery and Reception age do not learn in subjects: their learning is holistic and they learn through everything they do, primarily through play and explorations – both physical and with ideas. They learn throughout the day, regardless and often, in spite of what adults may be doing or have planned! Observation reveals how the child is applying her/his skills and knowledge and the particular interests, skills and understanding the child is developing but has not yet mastered.

The observation, assessment and planning cycle

Figure 3.1 shows how observations are analysed to make assessments and how all of this is used to inform teaching. It is expressed here as a continuous cycle, but of course is more like a spiral, as once one cycle is completed it moves continuously on to the next cycle in an ongoing cyclical movement.

The observation, assessment and planning cycle

The starting point
Observing.
Discussing with
parents.

Making it happen
Implementing the plans.

Analysing your observations
How is the child learning?
What is the child learning?
Deciding what next.

**Planning opportunities
and possibilities**
Through continuous
provision, activities,
experiences...

(Adapted from Hutchin 2007)

Figure 3.1

Assessment for learning

Formative assessment is sometimes called 'Assessment *for* Learning' (AfL), in contrast to summative assessment, which is the assessment *of* learning. It is usually defined as:

> 'the process of seeking and interpreting evidence for use by learners and their teachers to decide where the learners are in their learning, where they need to go and how best to get there.' (Assessment Reform Group, 2002)

The Assessment Reform Group produced a set of ten principles for effective assessment for learning. In brief, these are that Assessment for Learning ...

1. is part of effective planning of teaching and learning;
2. focuses on how students learn;

3. is central to classroom practice;
4. is a key professional skill;
5. is sensitive and constructive;
6. fosters motivation;
7. promotes understanding of goals and criteria;
8. helps learners know how to improve;
9. develops the capacity for self-assessment;
10. recognises all educational achievement.

Assessment for learning with older children differs in several respects from that in the early years, but most of the principles are the same. However, one is significantly different, because of what we know about effective pedagogy in the early years. The full statement for the Assessment for Learning Principle 7 is:

> 'Assessment for learning should promote commitment to learning goals and a shared understanding of the criteria by which they are assessed.'

For primary school children in Key Stages 1 and 2, for example, this is usually taken to mean: sharing learning intentions with the children; helping children to recognise the goals for which they are aiming; involving children in self- and peer assessment; giving feedback and helping children to identify their next steps.

However, because of the importance of play and child-initiated activities in young children's learning, assessment for learning in the early years differs considerably from assessment for learning with other age groups in this respect. In play, the child is in control: the goal cannot be set by the adult. The learning intentions and goals are the child's not the practitioner's. Nevertheless, practitioners should be talking with the children about what was observed after the event and giving feedback without interrupting their play. Identifying next steps with them is just as important in the early years as with other ages. These kinds of discussions with children about their learning are very powerful, helping the children to see themselves as learners. We discuss this further in Chapter 6.

Too much time spent on paperwork?

The Tickell review noted that some practitioners throughout the early years sector were concerned about the amount of 'paperwork' they felt required to do as part of their record keeping on children's learning and progress. Whilst acknowledging that this was only an issue for some people, others felt that this was drawing them away from interacting with the children. The review made a recommendation to keep 'paperwork' to a minimum whilst still requiring that formative assessment remains based on observation, as it always has been in the early years.

What do we *need* to know about each child's learning?

On courses I have run for teachers and practitioners about assessment in the early years, all over England, I have asked the participants what they feel they really *need to know* about young children's learning and development in order to ensure their teaching is effective. The question I ask is simple – there is no preamble to it which might result in a skewed answer. Interestingly, the answers are usually very similar:

▸ How the children are learning

▸ What interests them? What makes them tick? What triggers and motivates them?

▸ Their likes and dislikes: what makes learning fun for them?

▸ How is their emotional wellbeing

▸ Their learning styles

▸ Their decision making – the routes they choose

▸ How they make connections

▸ Parents' views

▸ Are they challenging themselves or does what they do appear to be at the level of routine action?

▸ Relationships and social skills

▸ How they are communicating

▸ What can they do? What do they already know?

As we can see, the emphasis is on how the children are learning rather than what they have learnt. There is no mention of 'curriculum areas'. Most of the points raised can only be seen through observing and listening to the children. The 'paperwork' issue highlighted by the

Tickell review and repeated in the 2012 EYFS Statutory Framework is a valid point, particularly about the amount some practitioners feel that they have to write down. The solution lies in finding the best approach to gathering the most useful information through observing and putting this to good use in supporting teaching: the topic of Chapters 7 and 8. The example here shows how one setting has worked out an effective way of making use of observations.

Effective practice in action

In this Early Years Foundation Stage Unit in a primary school, the staff team tune in to each child by first finding out about them before they attend, from their parents. At the beginning of the year they ensure there is time to talk to each child's parent, finding out more about the child. The close partnerships they build with the parents mean an easy flow of information about the child at home for the staff, and for the parents, about the child at school. The staff observe children as they work and interact with them, as a part of normal day-to-day practice. Assessment is an integral part of practice. They note down some of the things they see the children do which seem to be significant developments in their learning – the things they have not seen them do before. They talk to the children about their fascinations and interests and about their learning too.

In these ways they pick up the skills the children have already achieved, the concepts they have understood, as well as the ideas and skills they are beginning to grasp. All of this is used to shape the way they respond to the children moment by moment, using this information to guide their teaching. It shapes the weekly planning. The staff team are well aware of the importance of what they observe to their future plans, and how their teaching might miss the mark without it.

Together the staff have developed ways of documenting each child's learning which includes the child's own views, the views of their parents and the observations the staff have made in photographic and written form. Not everything is noted down, only the most significant. These are stored in wonderful 'achievement' books, openly accessible in the classroom, celebrating the children's achievements. They are frequently picked up by the children and referred to frequently by staff and parents.

The daily evaluations and weekly planning meetings begin with questions such as *'What made the children buzz today?'*, *'What engaged them most in learning and puzzling things out?'* as well as *'What didn't seem to go so well?'*, *'Which children didn't seem so engaged today?'* and finally they decide, partly on the basis of what has happened: *'What do we need to plan next?'*

Figure 3.2 This child is totally engaged in reviewing his own learning and development, noting his progress and comparing what he could do then with what he can do now

Summative assessment

When many people think of assessment, they often think of assessment *OF* learning, or summative assessment, rather than the formative assessment we have been discussing so far. In the EYFS there are two mandatory summative assessments: the Early Years Foundation Stage Profile which has existed since 2003 and a 'progress check' at age two which was introduced in 2012. As both of these are summative assessments, they provide an assessment of learning at a point in time. The progress check is not included here, as it is only applicable to children between the ages of two and three years.

A summative assessment can either be a test, exam or set task or it can be teacher assessment, a summary made at a point in time by the teacher. In the EYFS, however, it is based on the ongoing evidence of the child's learning and development, collected over time.

The EYFS Profile

When the Profile was first introduced in 2003 it was certainly innovative. Reception teachers were asked to complete assessments in the final term of the Reception year on all aspects of all areas of learning, based on their own observations of the children. There were (and still are!) *no* tests and *no* set tasks. It was, and is, based entirely on teacher assessment from their accumulated observations collected over time. And what might even be considered revolutionary, teachers are asked to involve *parents'* views of what their child is doing at home in the assessments they make. At the time that the Foundation Stage Profile was first introduced, all other statutory assessments in England for other age groups involved unseen tests and assessment tasks, even for Key Stage 1.

However, some teachers found the Foundation Stage Profile (and later, the Early Years Foundation Stage Profile) difficult to manage and cumbersome in its effort to cover so much. The revised 2012 EYFS statutory framework slimmed the Profile into a more straightforward assessment against each of the new seventeen Early Learning Goals. In addition, Reception teachers are asked to provide information as to *how* the children have been learning – a welcome addition to the Profile – in order that Year 1 teachers are fully aware of the strategies which have helped, thereby enabling them to provide continuity for the children.

All schools and settings who carry out the Profile must supplement the Profile assessment report

❛ *with a short commentary on each child's skills and abilities in relation to the three key characteristics of effective learning. These should inform a dialogue between Reception and Year 1 teachers about each child's stage of development and learning needs and assist with the planning of activities in Year 1.* ❜

(EYFS, 2012)

The EYFS Profile Handbook provides non-statutory guidance.

We end this chapter with another dragon story. Here is Mia's story – quite different from Louis's in the last chapter. Like all the dragon stories, these were used as part of the collected evidence of learning for the children, in relation to many aspects of both the how and what of the children's learning.

Mia's dragon story

Once upon a time there was a fierce fire-breathing dragon. A princess lived in the castle. The dragon blew fire onto the castle. The princess was trapped inside.

But luckily there was a hole in the castle. The princess climbed out of the castle and down the ladder.

A knight came to rescue the castle and fighted the dragon. The dragon flied off and they lived happily ever after. The end.

Reflection

Have a discussion with others in your school (for example, the early years team) about what you feel you *really* need to know about each child's learning and development in order to ensure teaching is effective. When thinking about manageability of assessment processes, check if you are gathering the most useful evidence through your observations.

4 From principles into practice

> **6** Assessment which is explicitly designed to promote learning is the simple, most powerful tool we have for both raising standards and empowering lifelong learners. **9**
>
> (Assessment Reform Group, 1999)

From principles to practice: valuing and supporting learning through assessment

In this chapter I set out the principles I believe underpin effective assessment practice in the early years. A set of principles on which to base policy and practice in assessment is essential to share with the staff team, particularly at times of change – for example when new staff are joining the team, or when changes in policy and practice are afoot. These help to establish a collective way of working and provide a basis for regularly reviewing practice: *Does what we do meet our underpinning principles?*

In three of my previous books I have also provided a set of principles for assessment. The wording of the ten principles has changed slightly from previous versions but in essence they remain the same. These principles pre-date the EYFS, but many are now echoed in the EYFS requirements for assessment.

Even though the principles were in my previous books, the explanations and examples which help to clarify them are new, partly arising from discussions with members of the early years consultant team and headteachers in Brighton and Hove.

Principle 1

The starting point for assessment is the child, *NOT* a predetermined list of skills against which a child is marked.

As Figure 3.1 (page 40) shows, the starting point to assessment in the early years is observing the children and discussions with parents. The *Development Matters 2012* guidance makes it very clear that the 'Unique Child (observing what a child is learning)' statements should not be used as a predetermined list of skills against which a child is marked. At the bottom of every page in *Development Matters* there is a statement which tells us:

> *Children develop at their own rates, and in their own ways. The development statements and their order should not be taken as necessary steps for individual children. They should not be used as checklists. The age/stage bands overlap because these are not fixed age boundaries but suggest a typical range of development.*

(Early Education, 2012)

Observations of children in play and child-initiated activities are the most useful, and through these you will find out so much about the child's real achievements. A predetermined list of skills will not help us to understand what we see. Any observation is bound to provide evidence of a child's achievements in many different aspects of development, but trying to match exactly what you see against any specific *Development Matters* statement will not do justice to the child's achievements. As an example, here is a child involved in a self-chosen activity in Reception early in the Autumn term, documented by her teacher as a Learning Story.

A Learning Story

Chloe Jade is painting at the easel. *'I'm doing the seaside,'* she tells her teacher. *'That's the sky, that's the sea and that's the car falling in the sea,'* she laughs. She has painted the sky at the top, the sea at the bottom and other items in the middle. *'I'm going to do the sun as well!' 'The sea is really bumpy.'* She has painted wavy lines. Brandon comes to see her painting and says *'That's really nice!' 'Thanks, Brand!'* she says to him. *'Look, look I done a letter P!'* As she continues to paint, the sky is covered up, the sea is covered up, the car is covered up and the P is covered up. The paper is now covered with a new layer of paint. *'Look now,'* says Chloe, *'It's great!'*

The teacher's photographs accompanying the observation help to tell the story.

The only reason this observation was documented was because the teacher (and child) thought it was significant and worth recording. Many aspects of learning were evident, including *how* Chloe Jade was learning through exploration, creativity, thinking critically, and enjoying her own achievements and enjoying sharing these. Her teacher also noted achievement in aspects of PSED, Communication and Language, Literacy, Mathematics and Understanding the World as well as Expressive Arts and Design. Going to the *Development Matters* 'Unique Child' statements in the areas of learning, to find ones which match the richness of what the Learning Story documented, is likely to be very time-consuming and underestimate the real learning taking place. For example, statements found in the 40–60 month age band – such as *'Explores what happens when they mix colours'* or *'Creates simple representations of events, people and objects'* or *'Chooses particular colours to use for a purpose'* – do not do justice to what was happening and would result in merely 'levelling' Chloe Jade to a particular age band.

The best use for the *Development Matters* 'Unique Child' statements is to consider the statements when summarising a child's achievements from time to time – usually once a term. *Development Matters* should only be used to show 'typical *general* development' and for evaluating your medium- and long-term planning, not for analysing specific observations.

The **Early Learning Goals** are used as 'best-fit' judgements for the EYFS profile, which means looking at the statement as a whole and using your accumulated knowledge of the child (observations, conversations with the child, conversations with parents, etc) and deciding whether you feel the child has met or not met the statement.

Principle 2

Observations and records show what the child *CAN* do – their significant achievements – not what they *can't* do.

A written observation is a recording of what has been seen – it describes an action, event or moment in time. As such, it cannot be negative. But sometimes I see comments in children's records such as *'poor language skills'* or *'can't relate to other children'*. These are not observations, but judgemental statements, dismissing the child as in some way incapable. Such statements block our thinking and understanding. They do not help us to think what to plan to support the child.

The process of assessment needs to be the same for every child: the crucial point is to observe what the child can do and analyse this so that you can take action to support the child. If you have concerns about a child's development, analysing observations of what the child can do already will help you to decide on the support the child needs in order to progress. The observations will show the child's existing strengths which need to be built on. Here is an example.

'**Johann** has additional needs. Through talking with his parents and *through their observations* the school staff know well Johann's particular strengths and interests – for example, his interest in, and enjoyment of, stories and books and his love of painting. Johann *has been supported* in his understanding of the routines and patterns of the day, through regular reminders and direct teaching of particular skills. A fundamental aspect of the support has been to ensure he is fully included in the nursery day, learning with his peers within the rich and stimulating learning opportunities created for all the children. His language and communication development *has been supported* to ensure he understands what is said, modelling the vocabulary he needs to talk about what interests him and to express his feelings.' (excerpt from Hutchin, 2012)

We need to guard against a deficit model of assessment. Lancaster (2006) reminds us of the tendency to see children as a person 'in training', thus limiting our views of their capabilities and lowering our expectations of the children. Assessment should motivate us to plan what to offer next and motivate the children to try something new or keep on trying. Acknowledging the achievement, however small a step the achievement was, should boost confidence and self-esteem. A credit model of assessment makes us celebrate the children's achievements and provide support for the next steps in learning. Most of the observations and Learning Stories used in this book show not only *what* the children were learning, but also *how*. They also show the 'Possibilities and Opportunities' the children, teachers and practitioners planned to do next.

Principle 3

Observation is an integral part of the practitioner's day-to-day, moment-by-moment practice.

This principle means that, in order to meet the children's learning needs and extend their learning, as clarified by statements in both the Tickell review and the Statutory Framework, we cannot manage *without* observation: it is integral to teaching.

Observation does not just mean standing back and watching or writing notes as you work with the children – it is a far more subtle part of 'teaching' than this. It involves what skilful teachers and practitioners do moment by moment as they interact with the children – it is about being observant and listening attentively. In the National Strategies booklet *Learning, Playing and Interacting* (National Strategies, 2009), the authors write:

> *'It is in that moment of curiosity, puzzlement, effort or interest – the "teachable moment" – that the skilful adult makes a difference. By using the "observation, assessment and planning cycle" on a moment-by-moment basis the adult will always be alert to individual children (observation), always thinking about what it tells us about the child's thinking (assessment) and always ready to respond by using appropriate strategies at the right moment ....'*

In discussions on this principle with members of the Brighton and Hove Early Years consultant team, they came up with a useful '3Rs' formula to describe this:

> *'It's about **R**ecognising, **R**eflecting and being **R**esponsive.'*

And sometimes when what has been seen appears significant, a fourth **R** comes into the frame: **R**ecording. A team member added: *'But don't miss the opportunity to interact by spending time writing it down!'*

A teaching story: a focused adult-led activity leading to significant learning

The children have only been in Reception for two weeks and this is their first week full time. As a book for the week, Jess, the teacher, has chosen *The Very Hungry Caterpillar*, by Eric Carle. The photographs and documenting of this 'teaching story' meant that is also a Learning Story about Enya's learning.

There have been many activities about *The Very Hungry Caterpillar* during the week and the children are buzzing with interest – there is lots of talk and new or less familiar vocabulary (such the word *'cocoon'*). Jess's learning intention for this session was a handwriting one, on the formation shapes such as circles and straight lines so important for writing. In the book, Eric Carle uses lots of circular objects or circular parts to objects and straight lines and the children are invited to look closely at the illustrations.

The small group of children involved are given large paper on large clipboards to draw the caterpillar, or the fruit using circles and straight lines. **Enya,** however, approaches the activity quite differently. Already able to read many words independently, she draws her caterpillar using circles and lines and takes it further, using her memory of the story and the resources she sees in the learning environment such as the days of the week written up and displayed. You can see in Figures 4.1 and 4.2 that rather than copy the days of the week, she has applied her own already well advanced phonic knowledge to write the words.

Figure 4.1

Figure 4.2

Principle 4

Children's play, self-chosen and self-initiated activities are prime contexts for observation, as these are key ways that children learn.

The importance of play has been discussed in Chapter 2, and in Chapter 3 the importance of observing children at play and in their self-chosen and self-initiated activities was also highlighted. More than any other context, I believe play is the one worth observing, as this is where children are likely to *'learn and develop at their highest level'* (EYFS Commitment card 4.1). Observing play means that we see children's real capabilities, which helps us keep our expectations realistically high and to plan accordingly.

Another good reason for this principle is that when we observe a child in play or in a self-chosen activity, we see how their learning is holistic. It is not divided into certain areas of learning or development, but many aspects of learning are always in evidence – as can be seen with Chloe Jade's playful self-chosen activity at the beginning of this chapter. It is therefore a rich source of evidence of learning.

The boundaries between child-initiated and adult-led activities are not always clear cut. The best adult-led activities are usually *'adult-guided, playful, experiential activities'* (National Strategies, 2009), where children are encouraged and motivated by the adult to make it their own. The Tickell review put it this way:

‘ *When working with young children the exchange between adults and children should be fluid, moving interchangeably between activities initiated by children and adult responses helps build the child's learning and understanding.* ’

In this example, the adult becomes a subtle play partner whilst Musiq remains in charge in his play.

Musiq loves story books and traditional tales. He told his teacher: *'I really like that Jack and the Beanstalk book'.*

Sitting on the 'teacher's chair', he is playing with the puppets for his favourite story, *Jack and the Beanstalk*, playing at being the teacher. Other children are listening, playing at being the children, and a teacher joins the children on the carpet. Musiq says to her: *'I'm pretending to be you!'* She replies, *'Can I pretend to be you then too?'* He laughs at this idea. Instead of sitting down with the children, she walks around the book area, playing with toys and acting as so often he has done when she reads stories. Musiq looks shocked! She asks him how he feels and he tells her he is not happy: why didn't she listen to him? She says: 'Because I am being you and that's what you do when I am reading a story!' She then says: 'I am going to listen really well now!' And she sits and listens.

Musiq is satisfied and he gives out the puppets to her and the children so that the story can proceed. After this event Musiq usually manages to listen better at times such at group story time. The teacher's response helped him to think in a new way about being part of a group.

Principle 5

Observations are analysed to highlight achievements and need for further support. They are used for planning 'What next?'

This principle is fundamental to assessment for learning, as shown in the cycle in the previous chapter. This does not just refer to the written observations and learning stories, but to the moment-by-moment observations made by the effective practitioner and teacher as they work with the children in play, children's own self-chosen activities and in planned adult-focused learning events. The need for further support is key and must not be left to chance: assessment and planning are not about what the child *cannot* do, but what the child *can* do when supported.

Principle 6

Practitioners should consider *how* the child is learning, as well as *what*.

This principle reiterates the importance of noting *how* children are learning, discussed in the last chapter, as this is so crucial when considering what to plan next. We need to think about what motivates and interests the children. What are their passions? What is absorbing them, taking their attention and concentration? Do children have particular ideas and burning concerns they are pursuing which can be seen in how they play and approach activities? It means noticing children's deep ongoing interests rather than 'passing fancies'. These become powerful contexts for learning. On the other hand, if a child's wellbeing appears to be low and there is no obvious sign of vigour, motivation or enjoyment at any point in a session or a day, then immediate action needs to be taken.

Not all children show passions in this way, and for many the best way to find out is through talking to the children. Talking to them about their own achievements, in the way described in Chapter 6, is particularly helpful, as well as talking to them immediately after you have noticed something significant going on. Talking to Enya after she completed her writing (page 51) gave her the opportunity to tell her teacher the strategies she used. She had made the link between what she wanted to write and the resources she recognised around her. No one suggested she should do this – it was her own personal and highly effective strategy: *'They are written up there so I copied them.'*

Principle 7

Parents' contributions to the assessment process are central.

The Tickell review noted that parental involvement remains a key area for development nationally. For some of the research and some solutions to the issue, turn to Chapter 5. As one headteacher said:

> *'It's not about a paper trail, recording what parents say or asking parents to write things down. This might sometimes work, but it is really about valuing the verbal discussions.'*

Principle 8

Children must be involved in their own assessment and their voices heard, regardless of age or ability.

This is the topic of Chapter 6 and a core part of assessment for learning. If children are not involved, it means that assessment is being done *to* them and not *with* them – they will have no ownership and will feel disempowered.

> *'If assessment is something we perform on children rather than involve them in, then we miss the opportunity for them to be able to become reflective, celebrate their achievements and we are in danger of taking away their initiative in what else needs to be learnt or tackled.'* (Hutchin, 2007)

We also miss the opportunity for them to be involved in deciding on next steps. Listening to young children helps us to question our assumptions and raises our expectations of their capabilities (Lancaster, 2006).

Principle 9

All records are open, available and shared regularly with parents and children concerned.

Many schools and settings have devised wonderful ways of collating individual records of their children, openly available to all, but especially to the children concerned and their parents. There are examples in Chapters 5 and 6 showing how these are being used effectively to involve parents and to develop children's awareness of their *own* personal learning journeys, and in the process enhancing their learning further

One of the problems often raised relates to the manageability of records which are 'on show' at all times. If they are always openly available, is it acceptable that some children's records may be fuller than others and that some may not be up to date? To answer this we need to think about who they are for, and their purpose. I believe we make these records to share and discuss with parents and children as well as to support our own understanding of the children's progress over time. These days many of the observations are just photographs with minimal text, thereby reducing paperwork. They are an essential tool for children's learning, celebrating their achievements with them, giving them the opportunity not only to reflect on themselves as learners but to reflect on their actual learning too.

I am often told by practitioners and teachers: *'The parents and the children love them!'* If there are concerns around what parents expect these to contain and how up to date they are, then this is a question of communicating realistic expectations to parents. This is discussed more fully in Chapters 5 and 6.

Principle 10

The child's record of achievement should be regularly reviewed, summarised to ensure the child's progress is tracked and used to support children's learning.

This final principle is an important aspect of the assessment process and expectations for the EYFS Profile. The Profile is based on the accumulated information about the child's learning for at least the full Reception year, and before too. In addition, there is an expectation that all schools will track children's progress and take action where a child is not making good progress. However, as the quotation which opened this chapter says: assessment which promotes learning is the most powerful tool to raise outcomes, it will only promote learning if what is assessed is used to inform planning.

Here is another and yet again different, highly imaginative dragon story. This is Charlie's dragon story.

Charlie's dragon story

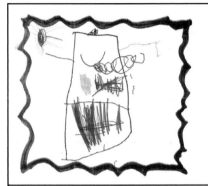	Once upon a time there was a dragon called Daisy. She lived in the trees and she liked to eat flowers.
One day my mummy and daddy went into the bushes to fight the dragon.	
(image)	They couldn't find the dragon but they found an old TV instead so they watched TV! The end.

Reflection

How do your assessment processes match with your policy? Can the principles outlined in this chapter help you to review and reflect on your practice?

5 Involving parents and carers

Principle 7: Parents' contributions to the assessment process are central.

Although the responsibility for assessing children in the early years rests with the class teacher and senior managers at school level, collecting the evidence for assessment is a collaborative activity involving all practitioners working directly with the children, parents and carers, any other professionals who may be involved and the children themselves. Parents may see their child very differently from how she/he is perceived by the setting, which sometimes results in a bit of scepticism on the part of practitioners. But this is precisely the point: to build a full picture, finding out about how the child is at home is invaluable, especially if it is very different. As one teacher put it: *'It's so great to hear what the parents think about their child. It helps give us a real insight about the child.'*

An area for development

Research shows that parental involvement in their children's education makes a significant difference to their outcomes. However, national reports often show that we are not doing well enough. In 2007, for example, a survey by Ofsted on the quality of Foundation Stage practice stated that *'Parents' involvement was an important influence in promoting good achievement'*, but that *'parents were rarely treated as true partners but, where this did happen, there was a discernible impact on achievement'*. In one-third of the 144 settings and schools surveyed, *'practitioners did not include children and parents well enough in assessment'* (Ofsted, 2007).

There have been significant developments since 2007 in early years settings and schools, and understanding of the benefits of a genuine partnership has improved. Many settings and schools have been involved in specific projects or programmes that have helped establish better partnerships. However, in 2011 the issue was raised yet again in the Tickell review. The review acknowledged that although *'many settings work very closely with parents and carers to good effect, this practice needs to be spread more widely and to become more consistent'*.

This was flagged up as one of the key areas for development for the revised 2012 EYFS, particularly around practitioners and parents working together to support their children's learning. So what are the issues?

Historically the tendency has been for a one-sided relationship between schools and parents in which parents are told about how the school operates and about how their child is progressing. But a genuine partnership requires a two-way process. To enable parents to be fully and genuinely involved in the assessment process requires a particular kind of ethos, which not only welcomes parents in all aspects of school life but enables them to be involved too. This sets the tone for their involvement in the assessment process and ensures they feel that their contributions are truly welcomed.

I have been in the privileged position of seeing some excellent practice in involving parents over the last few years. But in the training sessions I run for practitioners and teachers around the country participants often raise issues about the difficulties of getting parents involved, whether it is in day-to-day activities, special events, parents' evenings or in the assessment of their child's learning. The issue is often establishing a close partnership with *all* parents. Every child is undoubtedly unique, but so is every parent and every family. I believe part of the problem lies in the expectations and assumptions made on the part of both practitioners and parents about their respective roles in the children's education, which an inclusive welcoming ethos will help to address.

Developing an ethos of genuine partnership

Developing a genuine partnership with all parents takes time to establish, but the rewards are huge. As the Head of a Nursery School and Children's Centre told me:

> 'The key to involving parents is about being really clear to start with, so that people know what we see as important and they know what experiences the children will be getting. When we are clear about principles on which we base what we do, we can share these. This is the starting point. We need to explain the reasons behind some of the things that we do. It's then about valuing everyone's contribution and especially valuing the parents' input.'

Having an explicit policy for parental partnership which can be shared with parents will help to explain why the school sees this as important and how it works in practice. It also provides a benchmark for evaluating how effective the policy is in practice. The policy can be shared with parents at the initial meeting before the children begin in Nursery or Reception. It can be translated into the relevant languages and parents' views can be sought. It will provide an ideal opportunity to ensure that expectations of the parents and of the school are shared and that the importance of parental partnerships are discussed.

How parental involvement impacts on children's learning

The EPPE and REPEY project findings, discussed in Chapter 1, have shown that the child's 'home learning environment' is key to outcomes for children. In early years settings with a strong partnership with parents, outcomes for the children were far better than in other settings. The REPEY research (Siraj-Blatchford et al, 2002) noted:

> 'The most effective settings (where outcomes for children were highest) shared child-related information between parents and staff and parents were often involved in decision making about the child's learning programme.'

More recently, the EPPSE research reiterated these earlier findings. The 2011 EPPSE report included a study of the children from the original cohort, now in Key Stage 3, whose 'academic progress up to the first years in secondary school defies the odds of disadvantage'. In addition to showing that high-quality early years education continued to have an impact on this group of children, they noted the influence of parenting that 'facilitates and nurtures children's cognitive and social skills'. The nurturing environment at home helped to build resilience and positive self-concept (Siraj-Blatchford et al, 2011).

A review of research on parental involvement carried out by Charles Desforges and Albert Abouchaar was published in 2003 (DfES, 2003). They looked at research which covered both primary and secondary years, taking account both of what parents did at home to support their children's learning as well as their participation with school. Their findings showed that the most influential factor affecting children's achievements in school was what parents did at home with their children: providing a secure and stable environment, intellectual discussion and having positive social values and high aspirations. Children whose parents take an active interest in their schooling made greater progress than other children. In schools with similar intakes of children, it was those where partnerships with parents were strongest that the children did best. The implications are clear: parental involvement really matters.

All of the research mentioned noted that the improved outcomes were not only to do with academic success. but also with children's positive perception of themselves as interested, inquisitive learners.

Improving communication skills

Before we move on to some practical strategies, developing good communication skills is important if we are to form an effective, empowering partnership with all parents. This can be difficult from time to time, especially if there is a concern about a child or when parents and staff have very different views. Knowing the key skills of good conversation and being able to apply them will help.

- **Attentive listening** – Being an attentive listener is an important skill. It is all too easy when someone is talking to switch attention from what they are saying to what we think about it, blocking our listening. Being an attentive listener means paying attention to non-verbal communication and tone of voice as well as the words: yours and the other person's. Giving eye contact, and showing interest through your facial expression and gestures, are all important.

- **Giving information** – Be clear about what you want to say and ensure you give opportunities for the parent/carer to ask questions as necessary.

- **Time** – Giving time to talk together builds trust and reassurance. Pausing long enough to allow the other person to collect their thoughts is important.

- **Checking and summarising** – Once the conversation is flowing, and without interrupting the flow, check every so often that you have understood correctly. At the end, it is always important to summarise so that both parties are aware of the main points.

- **Asking questions** – Building up trust means listening more than asking questions and then only asking open questions.

Practical strategies and approaches to involve parents

The 'key person' role

Many senior managers and practitioners feel that the role of the 'key person' – the assigned person responsible for the care and well-being of each child, helping the child to settle in, and making the key relationship with child and family – has made a significant difference in building successful effective, genuine partnerships with parents. It has helped build a more personal relationship with parents and the children, providing someone who is accessible and available for discussion, clarifying the setting's approach so that parent and key person can decide together on the best approach for the child.

The 'key person' role has been a statutory requirement since 2008, and its importance is significantly strengthened in the revised 2012 EYFS:

> *Each child must be assigned a key person (a safeguarding and welfare requirement). ...The key person must help ensure that every child's learning and care is tailored to meet their individual needs. The key person must seek to engage and support parents and/or carers in guiding their child's development at home. They should also help families engage with more specialist support if appropriate.*

(EYFS Statutory Framework)

Getting off to a good start: settling in

Starting in Reception is likely to differ considerably from where children have been before and can be daunting for parents and children. Getting things right at the beginning is vital for child and parent: first impressions matter.

Home visits and visits to school

Many schools are able to offer parents home visits before the child begins. Some do this in the Nursery and others offer it in both the Nursery and the Reception class. Where this is possible, the benefits are palpable, enabling the key person (in Reception this is likely to be the teacher) to begin to get to know the child and family on an informal, friendly basis. Every setting is different, so when and how to talk to parents needs to suit the circumstances. So, whether the starting point is meetings at the school, visits for the child to the class the term before the child starts, or a home visit, it is the beginning of establishing trusting relationships between parents, practitioners and the child.

Involving parents in the assessment process needs to begin *before* the child starts in the setting – through, for example, a home visit and visits for child and parents to the setting. Often these are the times that parents are asked to complete a questionnaire which can either be completed by the teacher with parental input or they can choose to complete at home. It is an ideal opportunity to talk with parents about their involvement in the assessment processes, explaining to them why it is so important and the sorts of things you would like them to tell you.

Model questionnaire for parents before child begins in Reception

Child's Name:	**Name of Key Person:**
Date of Birth:	**Date of Entry:** **Age at entry:**
Languages spoken at home:	
Previous setting attended (with dates and number of hours per week):	
Names of family members/other significant people close to child:	
• Does your child have any particular favourite play at present?	
• What other sort of things does your child show interest in or talk about?	
• How does she/he respond to situations and people who are new to her/him?	
• Is your child used to being with/playing with other children and does she/he enjoy this?	
• What do you expect she/he will like about coming to school?	
• Do you think your child's communication and language development is what you would expect for her/his age?	
• Does your child enjoy books and listening to stories? Does she/he have any favourite rhymes, stories, DVDs or CDs?	
• Does your child enjoy and get involved in imaginative-type play and role play?	
• Does your child show interest in activities such as building or constructing, matching and counting?	
• If you have a garden which your child can play in, or when you go to the park, what does your child like to do?	
• Do you feel her/his physical development is what you would expect for her/his age?	
• Does your child have any particular fears or worries or dislikes we should know about?	
• Is there any more information you would like to know about starting in Reception or about our school and what your child will be doing?	
• Do you have any concerns or worries about your child's development?	
• Is there any other information you would like us to know in order to help your child settle and be happy?	

(Adapted from Hutchin, 2007)

Involving parents on a day-to-day basis

Planning the daily timetable can have a significant impact on the possibilities of involving parents and also in helping to settle the child in every day. It is great to see Reception classes where the day starts with free-flow activities where children and their parents can get involved together. Group time then takes place later in the morning and staff are freed up to get involved alongside the parents and children. This gives children an opportunity to settle, a smooth daily transition from home, and provides an opportunity at the beginning of the day, when children are freshest, to be absorbed in learning through self-initiated activities. It also enables the teacher to have valuable informal conversations with parents and the children about the children's learning at school and at home. This can form part of the process of gathering evidence about the child for ongoing assessment and planning. Ensure that every parent feels equally welcomed and their contribution valued. Over a period of time (for example, over two to three days or a week), make sure you take the time to have an informal conversation with each parent/carer who comes in.

Figure 5.1 Annie and mum sharing a story together

Not all parents will be able to stay and settle their child in this way, because of work pressures or other responsibilities. Some will be brought to school by childminders and some children will be coming into the classroom from a Breakfast Club. However, planning the day in the way described creates the right educationally sound ethos, welcoming and encouraging parents and children working together. For parents who cannot take their children to school, or do not have time to stay, appointments can be made, perhaps once a month or once per half-term at a time that suits them. Most parents can manage this, so long as the appointments are made in advance. Many schools now use texts or emails to keep in touch with parents, and these can be written in the classroom with the child on a day-to-day basis.

Making records or 'portfolios' open and accessible

Principle 9 in Chapter 4 is about making sure that parents have easy access to their child's record. These records always have different names! Sometimes they are learning diaries, 'profile' books, 'super books', 'all about me' books, 'significant achievement books'. For the purposes of this book I have called them 'portfolios'. They should contain nothing confidential and be always accessible to staff, children and parents. The best way to involve parents regularly in the assessment process is having the records openly available. Parents can then easily see the sorts of information that you are gathering and can contribute what their child is showing interest in at home through informal conversations, ideas and skills they are in the process of developing, and other things they have achieved at home but which have not yet been noticed in the school setting.

If the portfolios are available in this way, and the beginning of the day is a time for child-initiated learning that parents can be involved in, then parents and children can look at them together. They are not only important for parents to see but especially important for the children too (see Chapter 6).

I have never yet met a parent or a child who does not love these portfolios. However, concerns are expressed from time to time about the time it takes for practitioners and teachers to make them and keep them up to date. Plastic wallets inserted into folders are by far the easiest to look after and update. Everyone needs to understand that they are for notes and samples, not in themselves 'works of art' (although they will contain the children's works of art!). This is about sharing realistic expectations – that they will be updated regularly but not frequently and they are something which practitioners do with the children at school, not take home to do.

Figure 5.2 Annie and her mother are sharing her portfolio

Digital cameras, emails and texts

The use of digital cameras has revolutionised the need for written observations, and asking parents to take photographs of significant things their children are doing at home has led to much greater sharing of children's achievements with parents. Using electronic social networking such as emails and texts can also really work for some parents in providing information about what is happening at school or for parents to contribute information about learning at home. Some schools provide access to their child's portfolio online – particularly useful for those who cannot come into school regularly. However, this is not for all families, as some consider this way of communicating about their children to be inappropriate and others do not have or want these facilities. A whole-school policy in the use of mobile phones, cameras and electronic media is a Safeguarding and Welfare child protection statutory requirement in the revised EYFS. It is important that the policy is discussed and agreed with parents.

Home-school booklets

Teachers are finding a variety of relevant, exciting and motivating ways to link learning at home with learning at school. The EYFS Coordinator in one school, Robb, has devised a successful process of linking learning at home with learning at school.

'Our Significant Achievement Books is where we keep all the ongoing observations and photographs of the children's achievements. They are such a powerful record of both how and what the children are learning, which are open and available to the children who really appreciate them and the parents too. We want parents to contribute. What has worked best has been to develop significant achievement books for the parents to complete at home. A "home" Significant Achievement Book was given to each family to use over the Easter holidays. These came back to school providing a wonderful record of some of the things that the children and their parents had wanted to include, such as photographs and records of events.'

Other successful strategies for involving parents in the assessment processes

In my work around the country I have found that lots of teachers and practitioners find *'Wow'* cards and *'Wow'* boards, just in the entrance to the classroom, a particularly successful way of involving parents. Parents write up information about special things they have seen their child achieve at home and write these up on small colourful cards. Giving the parents a model of the sorts of things to collect is important – for example, something that made *you* smile or go *'Wow!'* The intention is that the child too is involved in the choices made as to what becomes a *'Wow'*. Parents and children may choose to bring in a photo or a child's drawing or mark-making as well or instead.

Recently one headteacher mentioned to me that when they put examples into their regular Newsletter to parents, this helped get more parents involved. But often, even though it may start with only a small number of parents being involved, once parents see what is happening, the process snowballs.

Sharing what has happened during the day

Many schools and settings are making use of electronic media such as digital photo screens, placing them in the entrance area or outside the classroom to show parents some of the most recent photographs of their children at work and play during the week. Some have taken it a step further and made use of larger LCD screens with live video link, so that parents can see the group session at the end of the day, or one recorded earlier, as they wait for their children. Parents are delighted by these and feel much more closely involved, understanding better what the Nursery or Reception class is all about from the teacher and children's perspective. This helps with parents' contributions to the assessment processes.

Sharing Learning Stories

In Chapter 7 we shall examine the enormous impact that Learning Stories, a particular kind of narrative observation, is having in some schools, helping not only to involve parents but also in reducing the amount of paperwork for teachers and practitioners. Here is just one example.

Annie, 3 years 7 months: Annie writes her name

Annie joins her key person at the 'writing' table, takes a chunky felt tip and begins to make marks on the small whiteboard in front of her. Her key person is involved with other children, but when she turns to Annie she sees she has written *Anni* and attempted to make an 'e'. She says: *'Wow, Annie, what have you written?'*

Annie: *'My mummy showed me how to do my name'* and she pointed to the letters saying *'A-n-n'*.

Her key person offered to show her how to do an 'e'.

Annie: *'I don't want you to help me!'*

After this she writes the **A** shape without the horizontal cross, all around the edge. *'These are A's,'* she says.

Key person: *'Where are the lines to cross them?'*

Annie: *'I do it after.'*

Then she went back to put the lines across most of the A's.

What did we find out?

Annie has chosen to write her name and to practise writing the initial letter: nobody has asked her to do this. Her mother has helped her by showing her how to make the letter shapes. She also knows the names of the letters in her name and she is pleased about her new skill. On seeing this 'learning story' with photographs of Annie writing, her mother was thrilled: *'I am amazed she has started to write her name. It's fabulous.'*

One-to-one meetings and parents' evenings

Every school has one at least once per term, but some arrange two in the Autumn term: one in the first half of term to look at how the child is settling and get parents' views, and a second to share the summary made for the term. This is a useful time for parents to have a one-to-one meeting with their child's teacher. However it does not work for every parent, as evening can be a very difficult time for parents with other children or who may be working. Many Reception and Nursery classes and Children's Centres prefer to arrange one-to-one meetings at either end of the day, planning the dates well in advance so that parents can make plans. These are important times to share everything that both parents and staff see as important about the child's learning and development. In Chapters 7 and 8 there are examples of how some schools and settings have made effective use of this time as part of their formative and summative assessment processes.

Curriculum workshops

Many schools and settings run workshop sessions for parents to support their understanding of how, for example, Literacy or Mathematics are taught in the early years. Some are able to make use of funded programmes such as Family Learning or have committed time and funding themselves to run more intensive programmes with parents on how to support their child's learning at home. The *Every Child a Talker* programme (National Strategies, 2008–11) supported the development of many settings and schools in running sessions for parents on supporting children's Communication and Language development.

In the leaflet produced by the QCA about parental involvement in the EYFS Profile in 2009, the Reception teacher outlines the processes she has set up for building relationships with parents. The school also holds regular 'curriculum days', inviting parents to stay with their child, to see how their child is learning and furthering their understanding of the EYFS. The teacher writes:

'We find that parents are more confident to contribute to the EYFS profile assessments following these curriculum days as they feel better equipped to write meaningful and relevant comments which will further support their child's learning journey.' (QCA, 2009)

We finish this chapter with another dragon story, like Charlie's in Chapter 4, where the child brings parents into their own fictional story.

Freya's dragon story

	Long long ago there was a princess in a castle. The name was Asabella.
One day the princess went in the forest and she saw a little blue animal in the sky. Then a dragon came. The princess Asabella cried and cried.	
	The princess was in the dragon's cave. The princess sneaked out of the dragon's cave. She ran to the castle. Her mum and dad were so pleased she came back. 'Where were you Asabella?' The end

Reflection

Reflect on the strategies highlighted in this chapter for involving parents in their children's learning. What do you find is the most effective strategy in your setting? Does it involve *all* parents? What more could be done?

6 Involving the children

An important aspect of observing and assessing young children is *listening* to them: their views about themselves and their own learning matter. Here is how one school involves the children.

Isobel, aged 4, is in a Reception class. It is the Spring term and she has been in school for just one term. The portfolios of observations and notes in this school are called Significant Achievement Books. Isobel's book is full of observations collected by the staff, including many photographs showing not only particular achievements but Isobel in the processes of learning. The books are regularly shared with all the children and with their parents. In this example, Isobel is being given an opportunity to think about her own learning. The discussion began when Isobel was asked: *'Looking through your book, which parts do you like the best and feel most proud of?'*

'I made this model with the blocks and then I knocked it down. I wanted to do it again, but I couldn't remember how to do it. Sandra showed me the photograph.'

Turning the page she said: *'This is my favourite page.'* She looks at a photograph of herself with a paper mask on her face. *'I made the mask all by myself. I did all the drawing on it. It's just got one eye-hole.'* Moving on to another page she said: *'I really like this too. Look, I made a mermaid. I cut out her tail and decorated it.'*

(Hutchin, 2012)

Principle 9 in Chapter 4 is about the importance of having open, accessible, child-friendly individual 'portfolios', readily available to the children and parents at all times. Sharing them with the children gives them the opportunity to reflect back and talk about what they could do before and what they can do now. Having the record accessible and available in this way, and talking about it with Isobel regularly, engenders a great sense of personal worth and achievement. She is clear about the things she feels most proud about.

The benefits for practitioners of such discussions are huge, providing an insight into the children's thinking, evidence about how they think they are learning, what they think about their own achievements and what they feel they are struggling to achieve. For the children, the benefits are about being able to express their views, develop self-awareness, raising their self-esteem and pride in their achievements, empowering them to reflect on their achievements and what they want to be able to do next. However, such discussions need to be planned, to ensure that every child is given this opportunity.

All the theory and research on assessment for learning stresses the central role of the learner in the assessment process. In 1999 the Assessment Reform Group put together the now-famous pamphlet on assessment *for* learning, entitled *Beyond the Black Box*. It referred back to the review of research on assessment for learning by Black and Wiliam:

> 'That review proved without a shadow of doubt that, when carried out effectively, informal classroom assessment with constructive feedback to the student will raise levels of attainment.'

Spelling out the research in more detail, they highlighted *'five, deceptively simple, key factors'*, four of which directly involved the children:

- *'The provision of effective feedback to pupils*
- *The active involvement of pupils in their own learning*
- *A recognition of the profound influence assessment has on the motivation and self-esteem of pupils...*
- *The need for pupils to be able to assess themselves and understand how to improve.'* (Assessment Reform Group, 1999)

One of the key findings of the REPEY research, this time specific to early years, noted the importance of formative feedback to children in the highly effective settings:

> 'Evidence confirms the importance of formative assessment to meet children's particular needs, especially formative feedback during activities.' (Siraj-Blatchford et al, 2002)

Talking with children about their learning whilst it is happening, or as close to the moment as possible without interrupting, is vital. But it is also important to give children of all ages the opportunity and space to talk about themselves and their learning, reflecting back on their learning over time.

I first discovered the power of involving young children in the assessment process in the mid-1980s, when I began to use a process for recording summative assessment pioneered by the Inner London Education Authority, called the *Primary Language Record*. The Record included a space for a 'Child Conference' and some guidance about how to carry it out. The target audience was primary teachers working with the older children in the primary age range, but it was not uncommon in London for teachers to trial this in Nursery classes. I never looked back from the moment I first tried a 'child conference' with a three-year-old, sitting on a pile of blocks in a corner of the block area. I realised immediately the importance of hearing the child's voice about what was important to them in their learning. Since then I have always believed that involving children in the assessment process is fundamental to effective early years practice.

Some practitioners may think that it is not possible for young children to be fully involved in reflecting on their own learning. But since the 1980s there have been many projects and programmes in the early years supporting teachers and practitioners in discussing children's learning with them. The approach is common practice in the pre-schools in Reggio Emilia, Italy. The 'pedagogistas' document the process of learning as it happens, scribing for the children, taking photographs and video, recording the discussions and the learning.

> *'It makes visible… the nature of the learning process and strategies used by each child…. It enables reading, revisiting and assessment in time and in space…'* (Rinaldi, 2005)

The Coram Family *Listening to Young Children* project (Lancaster and Kirby, 2010) examined ways of helping even the very youngest (under-twos) to communicate their preferences – such as giving the children child-friendly digital cameras to take photos or video of things which are significant to them about their setting. This project grew out of work by Alison Clark and Peter Moss, reported on first in 2001. The Clark and Moss research showed that many different techniques may be needed, fitting the pieces together like a mosaic. For example, in addition to talking with children in their preferred medium, such as home language, signing or picture exchange, the child's preferences can be observed, their portfolios or records and photographs can be shared with them. Many settings in Britain have adapted these processes to their own context. The examples in this chapter come from several different settings I visited in preparing this book.

Children's rights

Reasons for involving children in the assessment process are not just for the effect it can have on their learning, development and self-reflection, they are also about respect, rights and justice. The UN Convention on the Rights of the Child (UNCRC), which Britain signed in 1991, establishes in law the rights of children. This is so important that it is mentioned on the cover page of *Development Matters 2012*. Article 12 of the UNCRC addresses children's rights to express an opinion and to have that opinion taken into account, in any matter or procedure affecting the child. Article 13 follows this with the right to seek, receive and share information. There is thus a legal and moral imperative to involve the children in their own assessment.

Involving the children in self-assessment

Child 'conferencing'

The first step in involving children in assessment is giving them space to talk about themselves one-to-one with the practitioner. This is no mean feat in a class of thirty children. But it starts with believing that this is important, possible and worthwhile, then building it into weekly planning. Whether in a Nursery, Reception or Year 1 class, it means building in the time to do it. It may mean dropping other things instead, because it has such a powerful effect on the child's learning and development.

Children need to be involved at every stage in their own assessment. These are some useful strategies:

■ Tell them what you are writing or taking photographs of, and why. Show them the photographs. If it is something they are making, including mark-making and writing, they can be responsible for taking the photographs or choosing the best ones.

■ Make sure they are all aware of where to find their 'portfolio': have a special place for them.

- Talk to them about any samples or observations you or they want to add, telling them why you have chosen yours and asking them the reasons for their choices.

- Ensure they can choose their own things to add to the portfolio as well, but help them to understand that this is not everything, only certain things.

- Ask open-ended and inviting questions which will require more than one-word responses or yes/no answers, but don't force the child to respond.

- Even if some children do not respond the first few times you talk to them about their achievements, don't be put off. Continue. For most children it is the visual images which are important. For children learning English as an Additional Language this is particularly important. Children generally love to look at the samples you have collected and often love talking about their own writing.

Sharing 'portfolios' with the children

At the beginning of this chapter we saw Isobel sharing her Significant Achievement Book, taking pride in some of her achievements. Such conversations with children help teachers and practitioners 'get on the inside' of children's thinking, thus helping to plan activities which address their interests as vehicles to new learning. Here is an example.

Lewis spent a long time looking through his portfolio with me, going through it in detail, remembering the learning events in the photographs. As we went through it together, it was clear to me as a visitor to the class that what interested him most was the mathematical achievements recorded: the matching and sequencing games, shapes and numbers.

Having the portfolios available is a start, but it is only if they are shared regularly with them that the children are provided with the opportunities to reflect and self-evaluate. If this is to work for all the children, then planning for it is essential, timetabling yourself to have a one-to-one discussion with each child. Some teachers makes sure this happens twice per term per child, others do this once per term and some do it more frequently.

As you look through the portfolio with the child, make this your opportunity to make a summary of the achievements to date and think about next steps – a discussion shared with the child.

Some teachers also encourage the children to look at their portfolios together. Listening in to such an occasion, here are two children, Enya and Annie, looking at Enya's 'Super Book' together. The children are curious about what they have in their portfolios and it engenders respect in sharing each other's achievements.

First Enya talks about her favourite examples (see Figure 6.1 and page 83).

'Look what I have written: that's a giraffe and this is when I wrote some signs to help Mrs Snell.' 'That one says: I see Annie looking at me,' Enya reads and Annie laughs. Then Enya turns to a painting she made a while before. *'I like this one best,'* she says. Annie says: *'I like it too. But why are there those little dots there?'* Enya: *'I just splashed and splashed!'* (See Figure 6.2.)

Figure 6.1 Enya's giraffe

Figure 6.2 Enya's pattern-making painting, her favourite item in her Super Book

In the next chapter we shall also be considering sharing Learning Stories, the most powerful way of involving the child in their own assessment.

Child 'conferencing': interviewing children about their learning

The 'child conference' idea mentioned on page 73 is really like interviewing children informally about their learning or, to put it more simply, discussing this with them. It is particularly useful at times of transition, so that the child's view of their own achievements can form a part of the summary to be passed on. Many settings make an opportunity at least once per term to have this discussion with each child. It can be carried out in a variety of ways suited to the age and verbal development of the child.

How to do it

It *does* need to be planned as a part of the teaching, or it is likely to be forgotten or pushed out by other demands. For children with additional needs such as language delay, and children in the early stages of learning English as an additional language, other ways of gathering their views will be needed, with the help of signing or interpreters or using the strategies mentioned earlier in the work of Clark and Moss (2001). The best help, though, is usually sharing the 'portfolio'. Once children become familiar with this practice and have a better understanding of the vocabulary in the questions, they become more able to reflect on their own learning.

Pat Gura and Lorraine Hall (2000) point to the need to introduce much more talk with children about their learning:

> 'If children's awareness of their own thinking is to develop, they need to hear adults using words like think, wonder, learn, teach, imagine, believe, possibility, idea, explore, practise, pretend, experiment, problem, decision... as they play and work with children. Adults who think, imagine, plan and remember aloud also help demonstrate the processes involved.'

Asking questions such as those set out below helps to introduce the vocabulary and concept of learning to the children.

Finding out what the children think about their own learning

Careful framing of the questions will be required, but the important thing is to *try* asking the questions – if there is no response, try changing how you ask the question. The following should elicit the kinds of reflective answers you are seeking:

- Looking through your record, what are the things you feel most proud of?

- What do you like doing best at home/at nursery/school?

- What do you think you can do now that you couldn't do before/ when you were younger?

- What do you think you learn (or learn about) at school?

- What do you learn (or learn about) at home?

- What do you think you are really good at doing?

- What do you find hard to do or don't like to do?

- Have you any favourite toys/books/games/videos/songs, etc?

Sharing the termly summaries

The early years teachers from one school in the example below write a termly summary of a child's achievement, including a short comment on how the child has been learning as well as summarising achievements in each area of learning and development. They do this on a rolling programme, making up to five children per week their 'focused children' and ensuring there is at least one longer observation in the form of a Learning Story (as described in the next chapter), or carrying one out if needs be. Then they write a summary.

To make sure that this is a record for the child as well as the parent, the summary is written as a summary *to* the child. This is helpful in the assessment for learning process, addressing every one of the four points made by the Assessment Reform Group in 1999, on page 72. Figure 6.3 shows some excerpts from Brandon's termly summary for his first term in Reception.

Personal, Social and Emotional Development	You have settled into Reception really well and are good at following the routines. You are very helpful to the adults in school. It was lovely to hear you talking to Chloe Jade about her painting, telling her it was really nice.
Communication and Language	You are very good at describing what you have been doing and how you have been doing it. You are also very good at remembering things we have told you, showing that you are a really good listener.
Physical Development	You like to set yourself physical challenges, like the building and balancing you were doing with Tobi when trying to make bridges. You enjoy PE and are very good at following the instructions.
Literacy	You are starting to learn about the sounds letters make. You can already read your own name and many of the names of others in the class too. You really enjoy using the writing area.
Mathematics	You can always spot when Mr Muddle has muddled up our number line 1–10 and are beginning to spot the mistakes from 10–20.
Understanding the World	You helped to make bread like the Little Red Hen and were interested in how the ingredients change as you mixed them together.
Expressive Arts and Design	You enjoy making 3-D models and the music and movement sessions when you are now beginning to match your movements to the different music.
How you are learning	You are very comfortable with adult-led activities and enjoy structured games. You are great at answering questions and tap your head to help you remember things We are helping you to have a go at child-initiated activities.
What next?	To continue to apply your growing phonic knowledge. To invite children you are making friends with to join in with what you are doing.

Figure 6.3 Extracts from Brandon's termly summary

On the form the school uses, there is of course a space for the parent and the child's comment. Brandon's mother was thrilled to see his development so far and agreed with the next steps. As Brandon looked through his portfolio with his teacher, he talked about all the things he felt most proud of: his carefully constructed model of a birthday cake with blue cellophane as the icing and bottle tops for candles, which he made entirely alone and was recorded as a Learning Story; some of his writing – particularly the numbers he had written; and the enjoyment he was having in building interesting structures with the wooden blocks with another child.

Figure 6.4 Brandon's letters with legs   **Figure 6.5** Brandon's numbers

In the next chapter we will move on to observing and documenting learning, particularly through Learning Stories. But first, let's see how Molly, in another school, one of the younger children in the class, told her magical dragon story.

Reflection

In this chapter we have looked at how to involve children in self-assessment, reflecting on their own achievements as they happen, but also in reflecting back on their own progress. How do the processes outlined here compare with what you do in your school?

Molly's dragon story

	Once upon a time, four terrible dragons attacked the castle. The queen screamed and the king fought the dragons with his sword.
Magic Molly came to the rescue.	
	Magic Molly magicked the dragon and turned it into a frog. The king and queen lived happily ever after.

7 Observing and documenting learning

In this chapter we look at the practicalities of observing, deciding *what* to document, and *how*, putting it to good use and making it all easy to manage.

Making formative assessment worthwhile and manageable

The concerns expressed in the Tickell review, the EYFS Statutory Framework and by some teachers and practitioners about the overload of work on formative assessment in the early years are not new. As Margaret Carr wrote in 2001:

> 'A significant issue for practitioners is that documenting takes time and the time it takes will be balanced against educational value. ... when documentation is enjoyable, integrated into everyday practice, useful in contributing to children's learning and in providing feedback to families, then the time required is seen as worthwhile'.

If observations are not making a difference to practitioner understanding of children's learning, and used to support and extend their learning – then why collect them? Observing and documenting learning should not only be useful, it should be enjoyable too. In fact, it is this which makes teaching young children so exciting: puzzling out what to provide next, on the basis of what we have found out.

What do we need to know?

The evidence we need to help us plan effectively is any new learning: something *significant, new or different* that we did not already know. We also need to consider *how* the child is learning and it is always useful to note how and what the child is communicating. This can tell us so much about their thinking, the concepts and ideas they are developing and how they are using language.

Observations

Observing is a key aspect of the teaching role as practitioners and teachers interact with the children, as discussed in Chapter 4, Principle 3. Only some of what has been observed will be written down, only what is needed. And it is always worth thinking: can a photograph be used to save having to write descriptions? It is often far better to use a photograph or video clip and then the only writing required is the analysis. As well as saving time, this brings the written evidence alive, especially when sharing with parents and the children. Children's own creative marks can be used in a similar way too, but as these tend to show the product rather than the process, it is always worth asking the child about what they did.

Figure 7.1 Enya's writing based on *Brown Bear, Brown Bear* (by Bill Martin, Jnr)

Limiting the 'paperwork'

I often see copious numbers of Post-its or self-adhesive labels (often called 'stickers' by the staff using them), which in fact tell very little about the child's real learning. Many settings use this as the bulk of their record keeping. But it is worth considering how useful they really are. Are they really showing something new and different that needed to be written down?

The 'paperwork' involved in observing should not be in any way excessive – there is usually no need for lots of different observations, but what is written should be useful. If you have particular concerns about a child – for example a child who you feel is not progressing well, is overly quiet and you feel has low wellbeing or is finding it difficult to make positive relationships with other children or finds particular times of day hard to cope with – then more observations are needed to establish what the cause of the issue might be. These will be especially important not only for sharing with the parent but also if you wish to alert your SENCO or a specialist professional. She/he may ask for particular observations over and above this if there are some concerns about development. Remember that you are observing what you see the child do, analysing it and then deciding – with support from the child's parents and other professionals as necessary – the best way to support the child.

Using a *mix* of methods to observe is the best approach to collecting the information, depending on what you are involved in at the time, but there is one type of observation that is essential as it captures so much of both how and what a child is learning. This is what I call a **focused observation** of the child involved in play or child-initiated activity. A 'focused observation' means standing back to watch for a few minutes only, camera and clipboard ready as necessary. Three to four minutes is often enough. I specify observing play or child-initiated activity for this because this provides such powerful information about the child's learning. It should show you how they are applying their knowledge and skills and the new concepts, skills and knowledge they are learning. If it does not, then is this a problem of the provision not being right for the child? If so, immediate action needs to be taken to rectify this. Is there more that needs to be done to support the child in play or in making choices?

A focused observation on each child does not need to be made very frequently. Many settings and schools carry out one of these per term per child (some choose to do this every half-term). Planning it into the timetable, so that every child is observed in this way over time, ensures that no child gets forgotten. In many settings and schools the **Learning Story** approach is used for these observations.

What is a Learning Story?

A Learning Story is a narrative observation taken when a child is showing interest, getting engaged in or becoming involved in something which seems important to her/him. It may be play, a self-chosen activity or a conversation, and occasionally it may even be an adult-initiated activity which the child begins to take further. It may be something which the observer/adult rather than the child sees as significant, because it seems to show something new and different.

Margaret Carr, Professor of Education at Waikato University in New Zealand, devised the idea of Learning Stories with practitioners and colleagues at the end of the 1990s and early 2000s. It was a new approach to early years assessment to go hand in hand with the New Zealand early childhood framework, *Te Whariki*. In her book about the Learning Story approach, she described Learning Stories in this way:

> *'The stories included the context, they often included the relationship with adults and peers, they highlighted the activity or task at hand ... and focused on evidence of new or sustained interest, involvement, challenge, communication or responsibility.'* (Carr, 2001)

The observer documents what they see and hear, in the form of a story. Not every detail – only what seems to be important. As Margaret Carr puts it: *'Learning Stories describe episodes of achievement'* and as they are recorded holistically as a narrative or story, they do not *'fragment the children's experiences'*. She calls the processes which the Learning Story involves the '4 Ds of assessment': *describing* (what has been observed), *discussing* (with colleagues and others), *documenting* (writing it up) and *deciding* (what to do next).

Learning Stories in the English context

Although the Learning Story approach in New Zealand is tied closely to their own curriculum, the approach is easily adapted to the EYFS and has already been used highly effectively in many settings (see, for example, Hutchin, 2003 and Hutchin, 2007). As schools and settings consider the implications of the revised 2012 EYFS, many teachers and practitioners are switching to Learning Stories as the main way of documenting learning, because of the richness of the information collected and because the Learning Story approach includes the voices of all those that the EYFS expects you to involve. The 'story' will include photographs, the child's own work, the child's view, the observer's (practitioner's) view and the parents' views. Often the practitioner's role in the event is documented in the story too. The children's learning and achievements are valued and respected, through sharing and discussing what was documented with the child. As one teacher told me:

> *'Sharing the stories with the children puts them on the inside of what you think is important and puts you on the inside of what they think is important too.'*

A Learning Story neatly combines observation with documentation, greatly reducing the need for short notes on 'stickers', etc, which so often only record things you already knew or things which did not need writing down. An essential element built into the Learning Story approach is the *analysis* of the observation: What does it mean? What does it tell us about the child's learning?

Many of the observations in this book come from the Learning Stories collected by practitioners who either have this approach well established, or are developing it for the first time. In one primary school Nursery and Reception class the Learning Story approach has become well established over the last few years, started by the enthusiasm of one of the teachers. The setting is now a Children's Centre and includes places for two-year-olds and has a large number of children learning English as an Additional Language. When I talked with the teachers about Learning Stories, they had recently changed the way they write up the Learning Stories to make them even more user- and 'reader'-friendly, by writing them as a story **to** the child, an adaptation which began in the New Zealand context.

'The whole point of the Learning Story is that it is something to share with the parent and the child about the child's learning. So, it makes much more sense to write it **to** the child – it flows better and makes it easy to read it to the child if you write it as "I saw you do such and such...". It has really worked well for our children Learning English as an Additional Language too, because it addresses them as an individual, which has helped.

'If we have observed a group working together we can get some significant collaborative learning stories, then it doesn't really work so easily to say "you" so we use the children's names instead. We call these Learning Together Stories.

'The staff are really enthusiastic about the Learning Stories. Everyone understands why we are doing it and they all agree with it. We are not prescriptive about each key person having to do it in exactly the same way. It mustn't become a burden – the person writing the story has to enjoy doing it for it to work. It needs to flow and if it doesn't it won't be good to read to the child or for the parent to read. So they do need to write it in their own way.'

In another setting which has recently begun to use Learning Stories as the main way for capturing and documenting learning, the full staff team are also very enthusiastic about this approach. All staff find them easy to do, enjoy writing them and sharing them with the children and parents – even with the babies and toddlers. The staff in this setting also write them *to* the child. As one staff member said: *'It feels so much more real to everyone as a record of an important event.'*

Practicalities: how the Learning Story process works

Capturing the story

- Look for a situation where the child is involved in playing or another activity. This may be in a group or alone.

- Plan your observation time (with camera ready), timetabling this into the week, aiming for at least one Story per term per child in the Reception class. The observation does not have to be for long.

- This is likely to mean collecting three Stories per week.

Analysing it

Through analysing the observations, you should be finding out:

- what the child has achieved and is learning across many areas of learning;

- *how* the child is learning, for example in relation to the characteristics of learning;

- your view, the parent's view and the child's view.

Deciding what next

- Sharing what you have captured with the child helps you to share with them the *'What next?'* part – the opportunities and possibilities.

- And as Margaret Carr noted: *'A central reason for the assessment is to determine whether the learning environment is working for the child or children: is it enhancing their opportunities to learn or is it constraining them...?'* (Carr, 1998)

... and implementing the plans from the story

The next step is to add the possibilities and opportunities into the planning. Many settings do this through daily evaluations, where the weekly plans are tweaked to accommodate new ideas emerging from what was seen, but some planning points are for the longer term. So:

- Will it be through continuous provision with or without adult support?

- Will it need to be a focused adult-led activity?

- Which other children would benefit from this too?

If for some children it is difficult to capture something which feels worthwhile and positive through their play or child-initiated activities, it is important to consider *why* this is so: this is the time to think seriously and urgently about the provision and the experiences you are providing: are they meeting the child's needs?

How to document it

There is no required format for a Learning Story. Over the years practitioners and teachers using Learning Stories have adapted and developed their formats to improve the process and ease with which practitioners can use them. Often practitioners want to type them up and present them well because they believe this documentation is an essential and respectful record of the children's learning and the setting's work, shared with the most important audience: parents and children.

However, they should not be written up away from the children or in the evenings. An important part of the teaching process is to document the learning *with* the children. Typing it up on the classroom computer in front of the children provides a rich opportunity for discussion and an important literacy opportunity too, as the children help compose and read the text and choose which photos or work to insert. It is also an important opportunity for the child to reflect on their own learning. As this is a key learning opportunity, timetable it into the weekly planning, perhaps as a daily slot or once or twice per week.

Even though there is no one way of documenting the story, I have devised a format which many practitioners tell me is helpful in the English context because it is clearly linked into the EYFS and expectations for assessment. The format includes spaces for the all-important analysis of the learning, the parents' view, the child's view and the link to planning 'what next'. I have found, like many practitioners, that unless these are written on the format used for recording, these essential parts of the process can all too easily be forgotten, making the observation and the Story pointless.

Storing the learning stories

Many settings use Learning Stories to show children's achievements on their wall displays, as they demonstrate the processes of learning rather than an end product, usually also flagging up the support

A Learning Story Format

What did you see?

As well as recording significant things you saw, record the child's level of involvement and concentration, signs of wellbeing and the social context – were others involved too? If possible, record what the child said. Include photographs of significant aspects of what the child is doing.

What learning was in evidence?

Prime areas: *PSED, Physical, Communication and Language?*

Specific areas: *Literacy, Maths, Understanding the world, Expressive arts/design*

Characteristics of learning: *How was the child learning?*

Playing and exploring *(finding out and exploring, using what they know in their play, being willing to have a go)*

Active learning *(being involved and concentrating, keeping on trying; enjoying achieving what they set out to do)*

Creating and thinking critically *(having their own ideas, making links; choosing ways to do things)*

What was most evident?

Child's comments:

Parent's comments:

Possibilities and opportunities *(what next?):*

Observer's name and date:

practitioners have given. Mostly, however, they are kept in children's own records or portfolios, accessible to all in the classroom – what Carr (2001) calls *'collections of work in progress'*. If printing them off is an issue because of the expense, then some settings keep the children's portfolios on iPads, laptops or the computer in the classroom, where every child has their own folder easily accessible, with their own icon on the desktop.

Sharing with the child

The first time the Story is shared with the child should be just after it has been observed, finding a moment to tell the child about it. Because the practitioner or teacher stood back to watch and took photos or wrote notes, then the child is usually aware that something has been documented. If it is to be typed up, this provides another opportunity for discussion, and finally once complete it can be read to the child.

Sharing with the parents

Sharing Learning Stories with the parents is an important part of the Learning Story approach, providing information not only of what the child has been doing but also *'a view of learning that was being valued and encouraged'* (Carr, 1998). The stories can be shared quite informally at the end of the day. However, as this may mean that some parents miss out – if they are working or busy with other siblings – it is usually best to make an arrangement to share it with the parent when there is time to talk. The settings whose Learning Stories appear in this book take the opportunity for a discussion of their child's Learning Story or Stories at the time of the termly summary, with parents' comments added in at this point.

A Learning Story: The treasure hunt

Treasure hunts can be exciting provocations for learning across many areas and aspects of learning and development – combining, for example, Personal, Social and Emotional Development, Communication and Language, Literacy, Physical and Mathematical possibilities with Understanding the World. Here is a Learning Story about Abdi Rashid which arose out of his involvement in a hunt for some hidden models of animals. Abdi Rashid is new to learning English, speaking Somali at home. The story is written to him.

A Learning Story: What did I see?

Abdi Rashid, you came into school this morning and sat down at the writing table to write, as you do so often at present.

After a while you went outside and noticed there is a 'find the animals' hunt in the sensory garden. Mala helped you find a clipboard and showed you what to do, then off you went to look.

You began to mark off the animals you found on your clipboard. You named some of the animals in English: we didn't know you knew the names! Mala helped you with the names of the animals you didn't know.

You found them all. You ticked them off on the board and you had a go at copying the names of the animals on the sheet too! Well done, Abdi Rashid!

You wanted to show Jayne what you had done. You seemed so interested in this that Jayne got a book (an encyclopaedia) so you could find out more.

As you looked through the book, you found out about other animals too.

And then you found pictures of skeletons and skulls and other parts of the body! Jayne helped you understand what the picture of the skull is – it's that hard bony part under the skin on your head!

What learning was in evidence?

Prime areas:

PSED: You were really confident as you explored the garden for the animals. You were happy when Mala helped you but you also wanted to do things on your own!

Communication and language: You communicated well, mainly through gesture, as English is a new language to you, and unfortunately none of us speak Somali! You also knew some of the animal names in English too.

Physical: You used your handwriting skills to make marks such as ticks in the boxes and copy the writing. You hold the pen so well!

Specific areas:

Literacy: You seemed very interested in the writing on the sheet and then in looking through the book with Jayne, particularly the interesting pictures in the book. You attempted to copy the names of the animals too.

Understanding the world: You made links between the animals you found and the pictures, not only on the list but in the book too. Then you got so interested in the other pictures of animals in the book and the skeletons.

Characteristics of learning

Playing and exploring:
You were keen and motivated to have a go at this activity. The animals were well hidden, but you found every one. You were very interested in exploring the book too.

Active learning:
You were interested all the way through this activity, showing your concentration, enjoyment, particularly at matching the pictures with the animals and in writing.

Creating and thinking critically:
Although you used little spoken language (as we don't speak Somali and you are learning English), you were able to communicate some of your ideas and thoughts to us.

Child's comments:

You seemed so pleased with your achievements. I am looking forward to the day when you have learnt enough English to tell us all about what you were thinking and what you wanted to tell us.

Parents comments:

We are so pleased to see what Abdi Rashid has been doing and his interest in writing and books. He does lots of writing at home too with his older brothers.

Possibilities and opportunities (what next?):

We need to make sure you can have a lot more opportunities like this over the next few months and this will help your learning of English too. You are showing so much interest in writing at present and use the writing area every day. We will plan some more activities involving writing for a purpose and things like this that you can do in a group of children too. I am longing to find out what you are writing. There is a planning point for me too – I must start learning some words in Somali.

From focused observations and Learning Stories to other observations

In the first few weeks of the child's time with you, you should have:

- a Learning Story or focused observation;

- information from parents;

- what you have observed but did not note down: your developing knowledge of the child.

This is the point at which to think: is there anything missing – for example, an aspect of an area of learning you feel you have missed?

If so, the necessary information can be gathered in a number of ways: this is when the *mix* of methods for observing and documenting learning, mentioned earlier, falls into place. The *Development Matters* 'Unique Child' column becomes very useful when thinking what might be missing, and the 'Positive Relationships' and 'Enabling Environment' columns help you to think about how to address any gaps in teaching and provision.

The following types of observations are often written on self-adhesive labels or Post-its to be stuck straight into the learning diary, although some choose to do these electronically as they work with the children. Photographs, as in the Learning Stories, can often be the most useful aspect of the recording, ensuring that all that needs to be written is the analysis of the learning.

- **Participant observations:** when you are fully involved in play, children's self-chosen activities or adult-led activities.

- **Incidental observations:** the 'catch as you can' observations – notes of things you have seen which seem to be significant, but you were not involved in.

- **Samples:** children's mark-making, writing and artwork, both 2-D and 3-D, can be collected or captured on camera. Once analysed, these are great to talk about with parents and the children, adding their comments to the analysis.

- **Conversations/interactions with the child:** a conversation can provide so much information about both the child's thinking and how they communicated.

None of these take practitioners away from that all-important role of interacting with the children. You will see in the examples a quite lengthy analysis of the learning, demonstrating how much can be gleaned from just a few observations.

A participant observation

Shannon, who is almost 5, is in a nursery school. Her parents, feeling that the provision was just right for her, wished her to stay on until she reached statutory school age. The school has made sure that her learning needs are fully catered for and have noticed her particular artistic talents. In this adult-supported activity she has chosen to make a mobile for her little sister. The idea for the mobile came from a book about arts and crafts and Shannon wanted to make the mobile look like the illustration in the book.

Making the mobile

A week earlier Shannon had been involved in a colour activity using water, blotting paper and felt tips, looking at how the wet paper divided the colours into their component parts.

What was noted: Shannon knew exactly how to make a cross with the sticks using masking tape. She used the hole-punch to make a hole and threaded a piece of wool through each hole. Without prompting, she fixed the loose end of the wool with masking tape and then looped the long end of wool over the end of the cross, twisted it to hold it in place, then stuck it on with masking tape. She uses the tape dispenser for the masking tape very efficiently.

She talks about her younger sister, who this is for. *'Her's bigger now. Her keeps getting out of her bed and coming onto my bed. Her had her two birthdays now.'*

She remembers how she decorated the circles: *'those squirty things with water in.'* The practitioner gave her the correct name (pipette) and reminded her that she made patterns with pens. *'And then the colours mixed together,'* said Shannon

What is she learning?

Expressive Arts and Design and Physical Development: Shannon is able independently to follow a design step by step, using her fine motor skills to help, knowing which tools are appropriate for which task. She makes good use of the many techniques she remembers well.

How is she learning?

The only adult support she needed was an explanation of the processes involved, and a few verbal instructions. The observation shows clearly her motivation in completing the task she set herself, her willingness to have a go, and persistence.

What next?

We will continue to support her development of spoken language, by modelling use of pronouns as we talk with her and giving her relevant names of objects and tools she is using.

A 'catch as you can' participant observation

Although this started as an incidental observation, the teacher intervention resulted in extending Jamie's original focus into some significant learning.

Jamie, aged 4 years 3 months, in Reception class

Jamie spent a long time 'stunt' building with the attribute blocks, building up tall towers one block on top of another on the narrow end. The blocks kept falling down. I suggested he tried building something using all the blocks. Jamie and friend did this together, then placed a dinosaur carefully on all the peaks of the complex building. The observation was accompanied by photographs.

Analysis: what did we find out? Such a short observation as this provides a great deal of information! However, depending on what information on the child has already been gleaned from other observations, there would be no need to write all this down.

How is he learning?

Playing and exploring: willing to have a go, exploring the materials; *Active learning:* high level of involvement throughout this self-chosen activity and persistence as well as enjoyment of the process and end-product; *Creating and thinking critically:* took on the challenge set in his own way with own ideas, shared with another child, reviewing and reflecting on success of the strategies used.

What is he learning?

Personal, Social and Emotional Development: able to carry out teacher's suggestion, enlisting help from another child; remained focused until completed.

Communication and Language: plenty of talk, negotiating the design of the building as they work together.

Physical Development: Well developed fine motor skills used to balance blocks, although initial building kept falling.

Mathematics: Developing awareness of properties of 3-D shapes. Knew names of most 2-D shapes. Lots of problem solving.

Understanding the World: Clear interest in designing as he builds, able to express this to another child, showing a developing understanding of the properties of shapes used.

Expressive Arts and Design: Used his imaginative ideas to construct with a real purpose – the whole experience resulted in an imaginative story being represented.

What next?

Provide more challenges for Jamie like this, in line with his interests – perhaps he and his friend could describe the way they made the building, and in the process we could talk about which shapes fit together and balance easily and which don't.

A conversation with the child

Arlie, in Reception class, aged 5 years 3 months, is looking through photographs in his Significant Achievement Book.

'We made up a game – a kind of football game. We had to throw the ball into a tyre. I got it in once. The throwing and catching is easy. You keep your hands together then down and flip the ball. When you catch it you put your hands together.'

How is he learning?

Being willing to have a go: willing to have a go at describing quite a complex skill; confident, positive disposition; *Enjoying achieving what they set out to do:* re-living the enjoyment of the original game and feeling pleased with his achievements as well as the challenge of describing it. *Creativity and thinking critically:* all three aspects in evidence. The game was Arlie's invention; he made links between the photograph and the actual activity, and able to recall (*'I got it in once'*).

What is he learning?

Communication and Language and PSED: Took account of the listener when describing the actions of the game.

Expressive Arts and Design: The game was Arlie's own idea, which he was able to carry out with a group of children.

What next?

Encourage Arlie to invent more games, this time with an emphasis on mathematics (numbers). Support him to write the rules and play the games with others.

Mia, aged 4 years 9 months

Mia inspired her friends to work together to create a large paper house together with doors, windows and a garden, each suggesting ideas and sharing in the making of it.

Mia: *'This is the pathway to my magical island. You have to get here by plane. There's a hole for sand to go through and you can have some jam in sandwiches. If you want to go on the ship there are wobbly steps to it, but they have handles to help you.'*

How is she learning?

Playing and exploring: with a group of others, being willing to have a go at initiating ideas

Active learning: persisted until completed and delighted by the achievement

Creating and thinking critically: used own ideas to develop something new.

What is she learning?

Communication and Language: Mia was able to explain clearly what they had made, making good use of descriptive vocabulary.

Understanding the World and **Expressive Arts and Design:** Able to describe the features of her design and the purpose of what the group had made.

What next?

Encourage Mia and her friends to make her design in 3-D materials (e.g. blocks, sand or clay), to extend creativity, support understanding of materials and shape, space and measures.

Completing the formative assessment cycle: implementing the planning

In all of the examples in this chapter, the cycle is only completed when the *'What next?'* points are actually implemented as a result of what was observed. Some of these points will be addressed immediately, for example by extending an idea or making further suggestions to the child or by explaining something in a different way. Other things may mean tweaking the immediate daily plans. Some things need longer-term plans and may have implications for the way a particular aspect of learning is addressed, or for the learning environment. We will look here at the immediate day-to-day planning and leave the longer-term plans to the next chapter.

Daily evaluations

Vivian Gussin Paley, the well-known American kindergarten teacher whose reflective and researchful practice has inspired so many early years teachers, describes her daily evaluations with her team:

'Every day after the children leave, my assistants and I clean up quickly so we have time to compare revelations.... We speak of surprises, seldom of certainties. We want to talk about what we don't understand and what has not worked out according to expectations' (Paley, 1991).

Evaluating what you do daily is crucial if teaching is to respond to children's learning, reflecting on what happened and what should be changed from the original daily or weekly plan. In a Reception class, with one teacher and an assistant who is not paid to stay on after school hours, it is likely to mean that this has to be done alone by the teacher, having already taken feedback from the classroom assistant about what they have been involved in and spotted during the day. All that is required is a few minutes.

The process of daily evaluation involves:

- Thinking back over the day: which children did I spend quality time with today, especially those in play or self-chosen activities?
- What do we need to change tomorrow because of today?
- Which children do I need to share observations or Learning Stories with tomorrow?
- Which children do I need to spend more time involved with tomorrow?

If you are in a team-teaching situation, gather together as a team at the end of every day for a very short, focused discussion. Now you are ready for the exciting things the children will bring to the next day.

Reflection

If you do not use the Learning Story approach or make 'focused observations', try doing some observations in the way described in this chapter. Then decide what you think and feel about this approach. Does it make it easier to share with and involve the parents and the child in the assessment process? If you are already familiar with the Learning Stories approach, are there some children for whom a Learning Story does not develop so easily? If so, why is this? Try focusing more on these children: is the provision right for them?

8 Summarising progress, supporting transitions and on to Year 1

Summarising children's progress

Making regular summaries of a child's development and learning enables us to reflect on how a child is progressing and to ensure their learning is being appropriately extended. Summaries fulfil a number of purposes – such as planning for the child, sharing information with parents, providing information about the child's learning and development for the next setting or class at times of transition or as appropriate for other professionals, as well as providing the basis for tracking progress over time.

How often to summarise progress is up to the school. Many schools ask their Reception and Nursery teachers to make a termly summary of each child's learning and development; some ask for this every half-term, whilst others ask for two summaries in the Autumn term and one in the other two terms. The only *statutory* summative assessment in the Reception year is the EYFS Profile, to be completed by the end of June in the Summer term. But whatever the timescale the school expects, regularly summarising progress is an invaluable process.

Over a period of time – for example, one term – you will have collected several pieces of observational evidence about each child. This is likely to include:

- at least one Learning Story or a focused observation;
- a few photographic observations and samples of work;
- a few notes you have made;
- information from parents;
- information from other professionals who may be involved with the child.

There is also your general knowledge of the child that you have not written down. All of this now needs to be summarised in some way. Some teachers use a format, like the one used for Brandon in Chapter 6 (Figure 6.3), which can easily be shared with the child and parent.

Many schools find that the most manageable way to make the summary is by choosing a few children's records per week to summarise on a rolling programme, spreading it out over the term (or half-term). This avoids the stress and overload of trying to fit it all into one or two weeks of the term. It also makes it possible to share the children's records with them in a meaningful way, as described in Chapter 6.

Summarising progress WITH the children

Make a time for each child to look through and talk about their portfolio or record with you. As you discuss the portfolio with the child, summarise what you are finding out. The best approach is to complete a summary format as you do this. It provides a wonderful model for purposeful literacy for the child too. As you do this, look out for the next steps you may have recorded which have not yet been actioned, such as 'possibilities and opportunities' from the Learning Stories.

Most of the schools I visited in preparing this book enable the key person to do this with each child in their key group. It provides such a great opportunity to reflect on the child's view of their own learning. Here is Arlie, age 5, looking through his Significant Achievement Book, giving much food for thought about his interest in large numbers. The next step for his teacher is to decide what experiences to plan next for him related to this and other points which arise through the discussion.

Looking through his Significant Achievement Book, Arlie said: 'My book says I can count to 100, but on the abacus I can count to 1000! How many zeros are there in a hundred?'

Sharing summaries with parents

Once a summary has been drafted, it is time to share this information with the child's parents. Most schools do this individually with parents through an individual appointment time, either at a parents' evening, or throughout the term once the summary is ready. Parents' views of their child's progress at school and at home make a vital contribution to ensuring your record of their child's progress is accurate.

Planning to meet every child's needs

Practitioners often ask how they can flag up concerns about a child's progress if the summaries only note children's achievements – what a child *can* do, rather than what they cannot do. This point is closely linked to that addressed in Principle 2 on page 49. Summarising the child's achievements is important and it is a child's right. If a child with SEN or a disability, for example, only had what they cannot do recorded, it would be unforgiveable! Be aware of what the child needs help to achieve from your analysis of the observation, and write this in a positive way such as *'needs support to…'* or *'nearly able to do this without support'*. Progress for some children can mean very small steps. Recording a child's achievements provides the starting point for the next steps. It also raises teacher and parent expectations of the child and helps us to think what would be appropriate to do next, building on their strengths.

Parents need to know what their child can do and what he/she needs help to achieve next. Enlist their support in helping to plan the kind of learning experiences that will motivate their child – for example, based on what the child is showing interest in at home to use as the starting point.

Every child is different and some enter Reception with advanced skills in some or all aspects of learning. Some may be well on the way to meeting some of the Early Learning Goals when they begin the year. Their learning needs must also be met, as for all children, through interesting, enriching, purposeful, playful and challenging but achievable learning experiences.

A smooth transition and continuity of learning is important for every child. Here is Fidel in his nursery school, soon to start in Reception and already reading quite fluently. In the transition to primary school it is vital that all his skills are acknowledged and built on. Parents' views are a part of this, building an accurate picture of the child's development. In the example below you will see what Fidel's mother had to say about his reading skills. She is providing vital information about how Fidel is learning. We can see how this relates closely to the characteristics of effective learning – for example, showing interest, being willing to have a go, involvement, curiosity and motivation.

'We have always had books for Fidel and read them to him, right from when he was a baby. He has always had a night time story. I used to take him to Rhyme Time at the library – it's a session for under-twos and he loved it. Also, we have the television on at home in the mornings to watch the news and he has always been really interested in it. By the time he was three he started to ask me what the captions at the bottom of the screen were saying. It is often just the name of the person being interviewed, so not particularly interesting! I would read it out to him because he wanted to know. After a while I started to just do it automatically.

'He is really inquisitive – about everything, and a real "trier" – he doesn't give up easily. Recently he asked me what the word "disengaged" meant. Where did he pick that word up? We were walking down a street the other day when a bus passed us, going quite quickly. He turned to me and said: "Number 23, to Liverpool Street". Not all the number 23 buses go to Liverpool Street! I was taken aback at how he could have read it so quickly!

'One of my favourite books is "Where the wild things are". He can read this now. We don't do much like phonics or with the alphabet. We do have magnetic letters on the fridge. At the moment he is interested in making words that rhyme, such as "pat, mat, rat". I was amazed – and he is really keen to play with the letters at the moment.'

Summaries at points of transition

A transition record needs to cover every area of learning and development and ensure that the receiving teachers and practitioners are fully aware of how each child is learning. The best approach is a simple format with a space for a summative comment about the child's learning in each area of learning and development, a space for a comment on *how* the child is learning (using the characteristics of learning), a space for *parents' comment* and *child's comment* and a space for '*next steps*'.

In addition to this, I always think that passing on a real example showing a child in the process of learning makes all the difference, helping to bring it alive, and making what could be a dry report come alive, reflecting the real child. The best approach is to ask a child which sample of their work they would like to include: this could be a photograph or a sample, which is annotated with the child's reasons for choosing it. Many settings also choose to send on a recent Learning Story or narrative focused observation, one which captures the child's particular interests.

Figures 8.1–8.3 show samples of work from a project with Reception children, reflecting back and thinking forward, and were sparked off by the time of year: the New Year. These are the children's New Year resolutions, the sort of thing a child may wish to include in their choice of sample to be handed on to a new teacher.

Figure 8.1

Figure 8.2

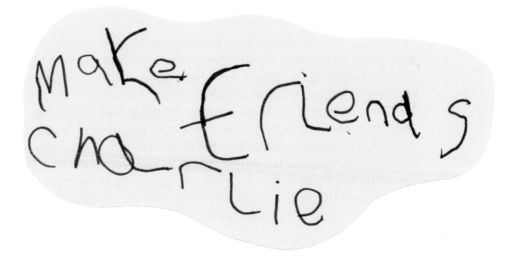

Figure 8.3

Tracking progress across the year

Summaries are vital for tracking a child's progress. In the next chapter we will be looking at creating data for a whole cohort of children, but this begins by looking at each individual child and tracking their progress. The previous chapters of this book have shown – with many examples from teachers and practitioners in a range of schools – how to collect the evidence involving parents and the children. But the final judgements at the end of the year for the EYFS Profile will only become manageable if progress is tracked *throughout* the year, in the ways described above.

Once a summary has been made, most schools use some kind of electronic system for tracking children's progress through the EYFS, and traditionally these systems were based on the *Development Matters 2008*, statements which were found in the *Practice Guidance for Early Years Foundation Stage*, pages 21–114. It is important to take note of the strengthened message on the bottom of *every* page in the 2012 *Development Matters* guidance:

> ❛...The development statements and their order should not be taken as necessary steps for individual children. They should not be used as checklists. The age/stage bands overlap because these are not fixed age boundaries but suggest a typical range of development.❜

This is important, and every school needs to ensure that their tracking system is fit for purpose and not burdensome.

Best-fit judgements

A tracking system based on *Development Matters* should ask for a best-fit type of judgement within one of the overlapping age bands for each area of learning. It should not check each child against each descriptive statement in the 'Unique Child' column. Remember that the child's learning and development may be quite uneven across the areas of learning, where children may appear to progress in leaps and bounds in one area of development, but develop and learn at a very different pace in another. There is no requirement to use *Development Matters* as the basis for a system to track children's progress, but it makes good sense to do so, as this is the official DfE-approved non-statutory guidance. It is the system that will be used and best understood by Ofsted inspectors.

Teachers often ask what they should use to track children's progress during the year, as most tracking systems hitherto worked by tracking which points were achieved on the 'old' EYFS Profile, with its nine-point scales in thirteen aspects of learning. This is *not* how the revised 2012 EYFS Profile works, as there is only one Early Learning Goal statement for each aspect of learning. There is only the statement for *'expected'* achievement: there is no statement for *'emerging'* and no statement for *'exceeding'*. This means that the most sensible way to track progress is to make a best-fit judgement from the *Development Matters* overlapping age bands, as described above.

Why track progress in this way?

Tracking progress has become increasingly important over recent years, but the prime reason for it is that it is an *entitlement* for the child to have the support and challenge they need. Schools and teachers need to know that they are giving every child the right kind of support so that she/he can progress to the very best of her/his abilities. Parents need to know that their child is progressing well too, and what support is being put in place to ensure they continue to progress.

> ❛ Practitioners must consider the individual needs, interests and stages of development of each child in their care and must use the information to plan a challenging and enjoyable experience for each child in all areas of learning and development. ❜
>
> (EYFS Statutory Framework, 2012)

This requirement sits well with what all those working with young children believe and it is at the heart of effective practice. It is about valuing the child, having high expectations and making learning fun, playful and interesting. It is about motivating the children and building their confidence in themselves as learners.

There is another reason for tracking progress – which is because Ofsted inspectors want to see data about it. They want to be able to see that the school is supporting all children well and they are making good progress. This means that primary headteachers and the senior management team want electronic data systems on which to track every child's progress from the beginning of their first year in school, including Nursery, to the end of Year 6.

Putting the information to good use

The information from tracking the children's progress is useful only in so far as it is used to inform teaching. So, having summarised the children's achievements so far and entered some information into the school's data systems, how the whole class or cohort of children are progressing should become obvious – but it will only show *general* trends. This means using *summative* assessment information for *formative* purposes. The trends may show the need to prioritise certain aspects of areas of learning, or show differences in achievements by gender for example, but as this is general and not specific to each child, the planning implications will be generalised – albeit often very useful.

Completing the Profile

At the end of the Reception year, in June every year, Reception teachers are required to make a 'best-fit' judgment on each of the seventeen Early Learning Goals, based on all the formative assessments that have been made, the accumulated knowledge of the children. If a child changes settings or joins your class during the year, then the Profile judgements are also based on any previous records, such as a transition record from another setting. As the Statutory Framework states:

❝ *The Profile must reflect: ongoing observation; all relevant records held by the setting; discussions with parents and carers, and any other adults whom the teacher, parent or carer judges can offer a useful contribution.* ❞

Teachers are just asked to make a 'best fit' for the Profile. This means taking the Early Learning Goal *as a whole* and working out whether, from *what* you know – written observations, Learning Stories, information from parents, etc – she/he has met the statement or not. It does not mean that every single element of the statement has to have been met, but whether the statement as a whole either closely fits the child's achievements or not.

❛ Practitioners must indicate whether children are meeting expected levels of development, or if they are exceeding expected levels, or not yet reaching expected levels ("emerging"). ❜

However, only the 'expected' statements are provided against which to assess a child: the Early Learning Goals themselves are the only Profile assessment points.

As it is a best-fit judgement, whether the child is considered to be meeting the expected level, or is considered to be 'emerging' or 'exceeding' in any particular statement, the actual achievements of each child will differ from one child to the next. Each will have their own unique strengths. This means that the information that is used to supplement the Profile judgements is of *key* importance to the child's next teacher and to parents. This issue is addressed in the EYFS by the all-important requirement, discussed in Chapter 3, to provide Year 1 teachers with information about *how* the child has been learning, through providing a summary in relation to the three key characteristics of effective learning.

The characteristics of effective learning

The statutory requirement is worded in this way:

❛ Year 1 teachers must be given a copy of the Profile report together with a short commentary on each child's skills and abilities in relation to the three key characteristics of effective learning. These should inform a dialogue between Reception and Year 1 teachers about each child's stage of development and learning needs and assist with planning of activities in Year 1. ❜

(EYFS Statutory Framework, 2012)

The information that is provided to Year 1 teachers through this commentary should give a clear view of the type of pedagogy and provision that each child has benefited from in the Reception year. This needs to be taken very seriously if there is to be continuity in learning for the child and a smooth transition to Year 1. And there is nothing to prevent anyone from doing *more* to help this continuity through what they provide for Year 1. As a Year 1 teacher told me:

'What I want to know about the children is captured best in Learning Stories or those narrative observations. A few of these tell me so much more about how the child is progressing than anything I can get from a summary or the EYFS Profile. I need to know about the child in action, how they have been when they are in school and from the rich evidence in the narrative observations I can plan what I need to do.'

Providing this will highlight the uniqueness of each child, bringing a written report alive. If the Stories or observations were chosen by the child, with samples chosen by her or him too, in the way described earlier in this chapter, this would provide the best record for the next teacher, to begin their planning for each child.

Transition to Year 1

Over the last few years, as the Foundation Stage (2000–2008) and then the EYFS (from 2008 onwards) became established and embedded in schools, the pedagogy and practice between Nursery and Reception has become increasingly well aligned. This has meant that transition for the children has generally been smooth and coordinated, changing incrementally as the children develop. This is not quite as easy for children coming from private or voluntary sector provision and into Reception classes, but the difference there is often more to do with the size of setting and staffing ratios than pedagogy or practice.

However, as we saw at the beginning of Chapter 2, the issue of transition in many schools between Reception and Year 1 remains problematic. The differences lie not just in curriculum, moving from the EYFS to National Curriculum, but also in pedagogy, environment and many other factors, including the ethos of the classroom.

In 2004 the National Foundation for Education Research (NFER) was commissioned by the government to examine the effectiveness of transition practice between Reception and Year 1. Their findings showed that there was much room for improvement.

> 'The main difficulties were associated with the introduction of a more formal, subject-based and teacher-directed approach, with less time for child-initiated activities, choice and play. Children's skills of independent learning, acquired during the Foundation Stage, were not always being capitalised upon in Year 1.' (Sanders et al, 2005)

The research included interviews with children – both those in Reception and those in Year 1. The results of this were very telling about the pressure being put on young children by an often inappropriate pedagogy and environment, as expressed in the following quotations from some children:

Researcher: 'What do you like doing best in Year 1?'
Boy: 'I don't like sitting on the carpet all the time.'
Girl: 'Yeah we just sit, sit, sit.'
Boy: 'Yes and it's boring.'
Girl: 'Yeah and we could be playing outside and getting some exercise.'

And in another school:

> **Researcher**: *'is there anything you don't like about being in Year 1?'*
> **First boy**: *'Being on the carpet for a long time.'*
> **Second boy**: *'Neither do I, because it's very boring.'*
> **First boy**: *'And it wastes our time playing.'*
> **Second boy**: *'It wastes your life.'* (NFER, 2005)

Recommendations made by the researchers began by highlighting the need for transition to be *'viewed as a process rather than an event'*. They listed factors that needed to change, such as the need for routines, expectations and activities to be similar between Reception and Year 1, and for Year 1 teachers to consider the needs of younger and less able children and to continue the pedagogical approach from the Foundation Stage into Year 1. One recommendation was that: *'The amount of time children in Year 1 spend sitting and listening to the teacher should be reduced. Year 1 teachers should be encouraged to increase opportunities for active, independent learning and learning through play.'*

Unfortunately, the findings have never been fully addressed at policy level, although there have been many developments in practice in many schools since then and there are some very good examples of carefully planned transition strategies which are supporting children's wellbeing and continuity of learning. In 2005, the QCA, who were responsible for the Foundation Stage and the EYFS Profile at that time, developed a very useful folder of professional development materials entitled *Continuing the Learning Journey*. The pack was sent free to every school in the country and many are likely to still be on a shelf in most schools. It remains very useful in many ways, especially the DVD material which shows some carefully thought out transition practice. However, the materials relating to the Profile itself are now out of date.

The pack spurred on many local authorities and schools to set up their own transition projects. I was involved in supporting some of these in different local authorities, usually involving several schools. The issues we looked at and subsequently developed were around coordinating routines, establishing child-initiated activities and play in Year 1 (not just once 'work' was finished, but seen as an integral part of provision for learning), the learning environment and the need for a dedicated outdoor space, and – most importantly – implementing a pedagogy related to how children learn. These types of projects were exciting and have resulted in some significant changes becoming embedded in Year 1 in some schools, improving children's wellbeing and educational outcomes.

Julie Fisher writes about a large, comprehensive and long-term project she coordinated in Oxfordshire, the Oxfordshire Transition Project

2005–8 (Fisher, 2010). The project considered many of the issues listed above to ensure a smooth transition but in particular emphasised a developmentally appropriate curriculum for Year 1, introducing more of a balance between child-initiated and adult-led activities. Both Julie Fisher and the teachers she quotes in the book make it clear that making changes to pedagogy in this way takes time: it is not a quick fix and needs time to embed.

Let's return now to the schools who have provided much of the case study material and observations for this book, hearing from Michaela, a Year 1 teacher in one of the schools. She describes how she helps to ensure a smooth transition for the children from Reception into Year 1, a process that has been highly successful in ensuring every child's wellbeing, confidence and continuity in their learning.

'In the Summer term the Classroom Assistant and I visit the Reception class and work with the children in their own environment, observing them and joining in with what they choose to do. It really gives us an insight into how they are. Last year we made this into two one-hour sessions, which was great. We plan an activity with them around a story book – a book that they do not know. Planning it with the Reception teacher means that she can follow this up with the children later on in the week.

'On another day the children come to visit our classroom for half a day and we follow up with activities around the same story so there is clear continuity for them. This visit helps them get to know our environment. We have the same areas available to the children as in Reception, so that is continuity for them too even though the layout and equipment is slightly different. During this visit they go out to the whole-school playground. This is quite a change for them, as they have their own early years outdoor area, so it is important for them to see and get involved in the big playground.

'In the same week that our visits take place we have a meeting with all the parents, so that they can come into the class with their children. Last year all parents came, which was great! I introduce them to the book bags, the idea of homework and how they will need PE kits as PE is introduced in Reception in the Summer term, but they only have kits from Year I upwards.

'At the beginning of the day we have child-initiated activities for about 20 minutes in the Autumn term. Parents can come in and stay with their child at the beginning of the day, working with their children, just as they do in Reception. As the year progresses we cut the time down so that by the end of the year they are ready to sit down straight away when they enter Year 2.

'We keep our records a bit like in the Reception class. Throughout the school there are "Learning Books" where a lot of the examples of the children's work is kept. In Year I we also take photos of their significant achievements, just like in Reception, and these are added to the books. The child's book shows progression across the year and at the end of the year they take them up with them to the next year group.'

In the next part of the interview Michaela talks about the meeting she also has with the Reception teacher, talking about the children's achievements and their EYFS Profile results. At the time of the interview the new EYFS Profile was not yet introduced, but she felt sure the process would remain the same. She went on to say:

'We start off the year by using the EYFS to plan in the Autumn term, but we are well aware that those children achieving above the expected level need something different and that other children may need specific additional support.

At the end of the interview Michaela told me:

'If we had them sitting down working the quality of their work wouldn't be there, so we never have the whole class sitting down on the carpet together until much later in the year. Most of what they do is in small groups. ... We can't under-estimate how much the children get out of their free-choice activities.'

Here is the last of the dragon stories. This is Aiden's story. Like the Year 1 teacher quoted on page 110, wanting some rich information which would tell him about the child, rather than just having to depend on some data, I think he would have found the dragon stories would help him to build an accurate picture of the children who wrote them.

Reflection

Look at the transition processes in your school between Reception and Year 1 *through the eyes of the children*. Ask the children what they think, and more importantly how they feel it could be improved. Then involve them in making the changes – a brilliant opportunity for their problem solving, building negotiating skills, their self-confidence and self-esteem – the list goes on....

Aiden's dragon story

Once upon a time me and Louis were asleep in our castle when we hear big stomping footsteps. It was a dragon coming to attack us.	
	We called our good dragon by magic. The good dragon swooped down from the sky.
The good dragon killed the bad dragon. Me and Louis lived happily ever after. The end	

9 Data matters

What matters about data?

All schools are expected to collect and make use of data created from the tracking of children's progress, usually from the beginning of Nursery (or Reception year if there is no nursery) to the end of Year 6. What schools need is a data picture of the whole yeargroup cohort: who is progressing as expected, who is not, and who is achieving beyond what is expected? The reason this has become so important in recent years is because Ofsted inspectors want to see that the school is helping children to make progress. It has never been an easy call for the EYFS 'department' in the school, for several reasons. First, the areas of learning and development are quite different from the National Curriculum used from Year 1 onwards. Second, there is *no* requirement for a 'baseline' assessment, as this was removed many years ago. Third, the processes for assessment are quite different. And finally, and most importantly, the pedagogy in the early years (learning through play and a balance of child-initiated and adult-led learning) is very different – although, as we saw in the last chapter, in many schools this effective pedagogy is moving up into Key Stage 1 to ensure continuity in the children's learning.

Data and work overload

In talking to teachers, senior managers and headteachers, one of their major concerns about the 'excessive paperwork' referred to in the Statutory Framework has been over the tracking of progress and creating data. Their concerns also have been about whether they are collecting this for the right reasons: is it there to help the school support children's learning and development, or for accountability purposes to Ofsted? The accountability reason is understandable – everyone wants to get it right – but more importantly it should be done to improve the quality of educational experience for the children.

A major problem has been that there are so many different commercially produced data and tracking systems to buy, as well as those produced by some local authorities, each requiring different numbers and types of judgements to be made by the teacher. Most in the past have used *Development Matters, 2008*, with its thirty aspects of learning and hundreds of statements across the age range for use in Nursery. Some have expected teachers to highlight every statement once a term (or even more frequently), based on their accumulated records and knowledge of the child – a well-nigh impossible bureaucratic task! Others just expect a best-fit judgement for each area of learning, or aspect of each area of learning, judging in which of the overlapping age bands the child's achievements fit best. In Reception, teachers have often been asked to track against the 2008 EYFS Profile's thirteen nine-point scales, making a disjuncture between Nursery and Reception.

The changes in 2012, brought about by the revised EYFS Statutory Framework, may help to make the collection of data and tracking of progress easier and less time-consuming, and involve less time in front of office computers for the teachers and more time interacting with the children. Neither schools nor teachers are asked to track *every point* in *Development Matters*.

The 2012 Statutory Framework clearly states:

> *Paperwork should be limited to that which is absolutely necessary to promote children's successful learning.*

By 'paperwork' we should also take this to mean sitting in front of a computer creating data. As Helen Moylett and Nancy Stewart plead: '*This section of the Statutory Framework might usefully be posted on the wall of every early years setting, and shared with any visitors who seem to be pressing for vast amounts of detailed evidence...*' (Moylett and Stewart, 2012).

Making data manageable and fit for purpose

The simpler 2012 EYFS Profile means that it will merely show which of the seventeen Early Learning Goals were achieved. In the last chapter I show that the best way to track progress, across Nursery and Reception, within the revised EYFS framework. Turning this into fit-for-purpose data means taking your periodic (termly or half-termly) summary of the child's achievements, made on the basis of the collected evidence from observations, etc, and using a best-fit judgement in relation to which age band from *Development Matters 2012* fits best with the child's achievements.

This should simplify the process and remove early years from unreasonable demands on their time.

The data *does* matter

Over recent years, data about children's learning in the early years has become more and more important, particularly for accountability purposes, nationally and locally. But it has also become very important to schools and teachers in their own self-evaluation, a valuable source of information to reflect on how well they are meeting the children's needs. Realising the potential of the data to show us how different groups of children may be achieving over time has got us all thinking much more clearly about our responsibilities to do the best we can for *every* child.

The national data for the EYFS Profile in 2011 (using the previous EYFS Profile, with its thirteen scales) showed that overall 59% of children were achieving 'a good level of development'. This means that they were achieving a score of 6 or more in all seven scales of the areas of learning, PSED and CLL (Communication, Language and Literacy) and overall they achieved 78 points or more out of 117. This was called 'a good level of development'. This sounds very complicated, but provided a useful formula which all those involved signed up to. But looking underneath the headline we find a very telling picture about strengths and areas for development nationally, which will have been replicated by a large number of schools and classes. We find that:

- whereas 68% of girls achieved this overall level of development, only 50% of boys did: a difference of 18 points.

- 62% of children who were *not* eligible for free school meals achieved a good level, but only 44% of those eligible for free school meals did so – again, a difference of 18%.

- when gender was matched with free school meal entitlement, we discover that only 34% of boys entitled to free school meals achieved a good level.

Differences in percentages between groups of children categorised by ethnicity are obvious, with some groups achieving much higher than others, and whether or not English is their first language makes a difference to achieving a good level. This does not mean, of course, that every school cohort is like this. Many individual children perform very differently and many schools buck these trends.

But lessons have been learnt over the last few years about the impact of quality provision on outcomes for children – and there is a great deal still to be done to ensure every child gets the best possible chance.

The revised EYFS Profile and data matters

Even though the Profile and the organisation of the areas of learning and development are now streamlined and significantly different from before, it will *still* be a rich source of data for the early years 'department' in the school to analyse. Data from the new profile can and should be analysed by the following criteria:

- How many (or what percentage of) children achieved at 'expected' levels, and at 'emerging' or 'exceeding' levels?

- Which areas of learning and aspects of areas of learning are children achieving best and least well in?

- What does this data tell us about different groups of children? What about gender, free school meal eligibility, ethnicity, English as an Additional Language, age (or term of birth)?

- How are the children on the SEN register achieving? For this, *Development Matters* or another form of assessment may be needed.

- How does it match with the *Development Matters* tracking used earlier in the year and, where applicable, in Nursery?

These are just some of the questions to ask as you analyse the data. In this way, as before, patterns of achievement for different groups of children are still likely to emerge.

Taking action

There is only any point in collecting the data if it is going to be *used* – and in the early years in schools this means using it in Nursery, Reception and Year 1. The first question to ask about all of the above is *Why?* Why are these patterns emerging? It will be difficult to map the data from 2013 against previous years, as the early learning goals have changed significantly, but important generalisations can be made. Is there a repeating trend, for example, which shows boys do not do as well as girls in certain aspects of learning – or overall?

Data may matter, but children matter more!

This book has primarily been about supporting children's learning, respecting and valuing their achievements and most of all loving your work with them! As Vivian Gussin Paley (1991) said:

'Whenever I think about children's differences my sense of excitement mounts. Without the uniqueness of each child, teaching would be a dull repetitive exercise.'

And here is one unique child, gaining confidence in speaking English, talking about what she has just been doing, which was recorded as a Learning Story by a classroom assistant in her Reception class. She is 'making soup' at the water tray, full of (mock) gem stones and blue water, which she has just commented on. 'I doing soup and cleaning up, I need to clean that purple one, clean all of them cos Mummy says.'

Other children (and adults) would probably think of other imaginative ideas this provision might provoke, but Sana is in control of her own play and her own thinking and her purpose is to make soup, using the gems, finding bowls to serve it out. As she looks through the Learning Story with the assistant, she simply says:

'I like that story and those pictures. Yeah – It's good!'

Bibliography

Early Years Foundation Stage 2012 Statutory Framework and Guidance Materials

Statutory Framework for the Early Years Foundation Stage, Setting the standards for learning, development and care for children from birth to five (2012) Department for Education.

Development Matters in the Early Years Foundation Stage (2012) published by Early Education, available for download or in printed copy form from www.early-education.org.uk. This document is endorsed and supported by the DfE.

Early Years Foundation Stage (2008) Department for Children, Schools and Families, available for download at www.foundationyears.org.uk The EYFS 2008 materials contains the Statutory Framework for the *Early Years Foundation Stage*, the *Practice Guidance for Early Years Foundation Stage*, a set of sixteen Principles into Practice cards and associated research and resources.

Tickell, C. (2011) *The Early Years: Foundations for life, health and learning.* An Independent Report on the Early Years Foundation Stage to Her Majesty's Government. Available to download from: www.education.gov.uk

References

Assessment Reform Group (1999) *Assessment for Learning: Beyond the Black Box,* University of Cambridge School of Education.

Assessment Reform Group (2002) *Assessment for Learning: Ten Principles,* www.assessment-reform-group.org.uk

Assessment Reform Group (2009) *Assessment in schools: Fit for purpose? A Commentary by the Teaching and Learning Research Programme,* University of London Institute of Education.

Bertram, T. and Pascal, C. (2002) 'Assessing What Really Matters in the Early Years' in *The Foundations of Learning,* edited by Julie Fisher, Open University Press.

Bruce, T., Meggitt, C. and Grenier, J. (2010) *Childcare and Education,* Hodder Education.

Carr, M. (1998) *Assessing Children's Learning in Early Childhood Settings,* New Zealand Council for Educational Research, Wellington.

Carr, M. (2001) *Assessment in Early Childhood Settings: Learning Stories, Effective Early Learning,* Paul Chapman Publishing.

Centre for Language in Primary Education *Primary Language Record* (www.clpe.co.uk/research/the-primary-language-record).

Clark, A., and Moss, P. (2001) *Listening to Young Children: The Mosaic Approach,* National Children's Bureau and Joseph Rowntree Foundation.

Clarke, S. (2001) *Unlocking Formative Assessment,* Hodder Education.

Desforges, C and Abouchaar, A. (2003) *The impact of parental involvement, parental support and family education on pupil achievement and adjustment: a review of the literature,* DfES, 2003 RR 433.

Dowling, M. (2005) *Supporting young children's sustained shared thinking: an exploration;* booklet accompanying DVD, Early Education.

Dweck, C.S. (2006) *Mindset: The New Psychology of Success,* Ballantine Books, New York.

EPPE (2004) Sylva, K., Melhuish, E. C., Sammons, P., Siraj-Blatchford, I. and Taggart, B., *The Effective Provision of Pre-School Education (EPPE) Project: Technical Paper 12 – The Final Report: Effective Pre-School Education,* DfES/Institute of Education, University of London.

EPPSE (2012) Sylva, K., Melhuish, E., Sammons, P., Siraj-Blatchford, I and Taggart, B., with Toth, K., Smees, R., Draghici, D., Mayo, A., and Welcomme, W., *Effective Pre-school, Primary and Secondary Education 3–14 Project (EPPSE 3–14) Report from the Key Stage 3 Phase: Influences on students' development from age 11–14;* RR, 202, Department for Education.

Evangelou, M., Sylva, K., Kyriacou, M., Wild, M. and Glenny, G. (2009) *Early Years Learning and Development Review,* DCSF Research Report RR176. Available to download from: www.education.gov.uk/publications/RSG/publicationDetail/Page1/DCSF-RR176

Fisher, J. (2010) *Moving on to Key Stage 1: improving transition from the Early Years Foundation Stage,* Open University Press.

Gura, P., and Hall, L. (2000) 'Self-assessment' in *Early Years Educator,* June 2000, Mark Allen Publishing.

Hutchin, V. (1999) *Right from the Start: Effective Planning and Assessment in the Early Years,* Hodder and Stoughton.

Hutchin, V. (2003) *Observing and Assessing for the Foundation Stage Profile,* Hodder and Stoughton.

Hutchin, V. (2007) *Supporting Every Child's Learning in the EYFS,* Hodder Education.

Hutchin, V. (2012) *The EYFS, a Practical Guide for Students and Professionals,* Hodder Education.

Kline, N. (1999)*Time to think, Listening to ignite the human mind,* Ward Lock, Cassell Illustrated.

Laevers, F (1994). 'The innovative project Experiential Education and the definition of quality in education'. In: Laevers F (ed.), *Defining and assessing quality in early childhood education.* Studia Paedagogica, Leuven University Press, pp. 159-172

Laevers, F. (2000) 'Forward to basics! Deep-level-learning and the Experiential Approach', *Early Years,* Vol. 20, No. 2.

Lancaster, Y.P. (2006) 'Listening to Young Children, Respecting the Voice of the Child', in Pugh, G., and Duffy, B., *Contemporary Issues in the Early Years* (fourth edition), Sage.

Lancaster, Y.P. and Kirby, P. (2010) Coram Family, *Listening to Young Children (pack),* Open University Press.

Moylett, H. and Stewart, N. (2012) *Understanding the revised Early Years Foundation Stage,* Early Education.

National Strategies (2007) *Confident, capable and creative: supporting boys' achievements*, DCSF, available for download from www.foundationyears.org.uk

National Strategies (2009) *Learning, Playing and Interacting*, available for download from Foundation Years website, www.foundationyears.org.uk

National Strategies (2010) *Finding and Exploring Children's Fascinations*, DCSF, available for download from www.foundationyears.org.uk

Ofsted (2007) *The Foundation Stage: A Survey of 144 settings*, Ofsted.

Paley, V.G. (1991) *The boy who would be a helicopter*, Harvard University Press.

Paley, V.G. (2004) *A Child's Work: The Importance of Fantasy Play*, University of Chicago Press.

QCA (2005) *Continuing the Learning Journey, Training materials*, available for download at www.foundationyears.org.uk/2011/11/continuing-the-learning-journey/

QCA (2009) *Engaging parents in EYFS profile assessments: a case study*, available for download at www.teachfind.com/qcda/eyfs-resources-qcda

Rinaldi, C. (2005) 'Documentation and Assessment: what is the relationship?', in Clark, A., Kjorholt, A.T., and Moss, P. *Beyond Listening: children's perspectives on early childhood services* , The Policy Press, University of Bristol.

Robinson, K. (1999) *All Our Futures: Creativity, Culture and Education*, National Advisory Committee on Creative and Cultural Education.

Sanders, D., White, G., Burge, B., Sharp, C., Eames, A., McEune, R and Grayson, H. (2005) *A Study of the Transition from the Foundation Stage to Key Stage 1*, National Foundation for Educational Research.

Siraj-Blatchford, I., Sylva, K., Muttock, S., *Gilden, R. and Bell, D.* (2002) *Researching Effective Pedagogy in the Early Years (REPEY)*, DfES.

Siraj-Blatchford, I., Mayo, A., Melhuish, E., Taggart, B., Sammons, P. and Sylva. K. (2011) *Performing against the odds: developmental trajectories of children in the EPPSE 3-16 study*. Department for Education. London. Available for download from: www.education.gov.uk/publications/standard/publicationDetail/Page1/DFE-RR128

Stewart, N. (2011) *How children learn: the characteristics of effective early learning*, Early Education.

Vygotsky, L. (1978) *Mind in Society*, Harvard University Press.

Wheeler, H and Connor, J. (2009) *Parents, Early Years and Learning: Parents as Partners in the EYFS*, National Children's Bureau.

Wiliam, D. (2009) *Assessment for Learning: why, what and how*, University of London Institute of Education.

Children's books

Eric Carle (1969), *The Very Hungry Caterpillar*, Philomel Books.

Bill Martin, Junior (1967) *Brown Bear, Brown Bear*, Holt, Rhinehart and Winston.

For further reading about Learning Stories

www.unisanet.unisa.edu.au/staff/SueHill/Learningstories.pdf

www.educate.ece.govt.nz/learning/curriculumAndLearning/Assessmentforlearning/KeiTuaotePae.aspx